THE TEACHING REVOLUTION

The
Teaching Revolution

W. KENNETH RICHMOND
Department of Education, Glasgow University

METHUEN & CO LTD
11 NEW FETTER LANE LONDON EC4

First published 1967 by Methuen and Co Ltd
11 New Fetter Lane, London, EC4
©1967 W. Kenneth Richmond
Printed in Great Britain by
Richard Clay (The Chaucer Press) Ltd, Bungay, Suffolk

Distributed in the U.S.A
by Barnes & Noble Inc

Preface

Hercules, it will be remembered, was an accommodating fellow, always ready (if not always wise) to turn his hand to prodigious undertakings. Only an intellectual giant could expect to carry off the *tour de force* that is needed in such an assignment as *The Teaching Revolution* represents, and lesser mortals who aspire to do so run the risk of looking merely preposterous.

When the proposals for the book were first mooted I had no idea that the task of writing it single-handed would be left to me. My original reaction was that any review of current educational innovations would need to take the form of a symposium, with authoritative contributions from leading figures in different fields. The publishers, rightly or wrongly, disagreed: in their judgement, the danger was that this kind of treatment would yield only a collection of essays, lacking cohesion and central purpose. What they had in mind was a synoptic account. My main objection to this – apart from the obvious one of its being a tall order – was that any single-handed treatment was bound to suffer from over-compression: in places, it would either be unintelligible to the layman or it would be too elementary for the expert. But the blandishments of publishers are like the way of a man with a maid, and in the end they had their way.

Upon reflection it seems that their judgement was sound – though how far they were well advised to commission such a person as myself for the job is another matter. More and more as the work proceeded I was impressed by two things: on the one hand, the fact that each of the significant growth-points in education – programmed learning, closed-circuit television, team-teaching, the 'New Mathematics' and the various curriculum reform projects – tended to be isolated from the others, developing on its own lines and according to its own lights without any overall surveillance; on the other (and it is this, more than anything else which has made the writing of *The Teaching Revolution* personally worthwhile), the realization that certain common features were emerging. If the thought that there was no supreme body capable of exercising control over all these trends seemed disturbing – disturbing in the sense that there was apparently no prospect of co-ordinating them in a policy, let alone in a master-plan – it was at least reassuring to find them pointing, however vaguely, in the same direction. Time and again, these common features kept cropping up in widely separated contexts. Everywhere, it seemed, the same arguments, the same approaches, and the same key-words – 'models', 'systems', 'strategies', 'objectives', 'taxonomy', 'structure', and 'sequence', among others – were being used.

Inevitably, as the reader will notice, this has led to a fair amount of overlapping in the ensuing account, and in places the argument tends to repeat itself. To attempt to impose a pattern upon the contemporary flux, as I have done in the final chapter, 'Outlines for a New Pedagogy', is to invite abject failure: only the urgency of the need renders it excusable. My indebtedness to Jerome S. Bruner – *il miglior fabbro* in these matters – is only too obvious. More than any other single individual, he has underlined the need for a genuinely prescriptive theory of instruction, the kind which 'caps, clears and clinches' all the premises and promises in our educational practice.

In the USA, where much of the preliminary work for *The Teaching Revolution* was done, the situation is no less confused than it is in Britain. I can only hope that the interminable discussions with my colleagues in the University of Glasgow and the University of Texas (not forgetting members of my Ph.D. Class 285) have gone part of the way towards clarifying it.

W. KENNETH RICHMOND

Contents

List of Illustrations

PLATES

between pages 60 and 61

Number work with Cuisenaire rods

Experiment in computer-assisted instruction: the new mathematics at primary level

Team-teaching: the nature of sound

Nuffield Physics Project: first-year experiment to find the size of a molecule of oil

Mechanization in the secondary school: desk calculators and an Autotutor

FIGURES

Acknowledgements

The Author and Publishers wish to thank the following for permission to reproduce illustrations appearing in this book:

IBM United Kingdom Limited
The Marconi Company Limited

Other photographs are by Henry Grant, AIIP

Acknowledgement is also due to the following:

Constable Young Books Ltd, for a quotation from *Experiments in Education at Sevenoaks*, edited by L. C. Taylor; the National Education Association, for a quotation from *Trends in Programmed Instruction*, edited by G. D. Ofiesh and W. C. Meierhenry; Hutchinson Publishing Group Ltd, for a quotation from *An Experimental Study of Mathematics Learning*, by Z. P. Dienes; J. P. Guilford for fig. 5; R. Glaser and J. H. Reynolds for figs. 10 and 11; and Robert F. Mager for a quotation from a lecture 'Setting Objectives for Programmed Instruction'.

CHAPTER ONE

The Teaching Revolution

Authors who elect to write books with intemperate titles do well
to explain their motives and outline their position at the outset.
Let it be clear, therefore, that in the ensuing discussion there will
be nothing to suggest that the Teaching Revolution can be treated
as if it were already a *fait accompli*, and that a very considerable
question-mark needs to be placed even against the possibility of
its being in the offing. To say that the organizational, curricular,
and methodological modifications now being introduced in
schools throughout the land can be characterized as sweeping
changes is to claim too much; to pretend that they add up to a
radical transformation of established practice will deceive no one
who is familiar with the state of educational affairs at first hand;
and to assert that they amount to an actual revolution is merely
melodramatic. Even in the USA, where these modifications have
been carried a good deal further and on a much broader front than
they have in Britain, the only sober appraisal of the situation must
be that so far as the rank and file of teachers are concerned it is
still a case of business as usual.

At the same time, while it may not be immediately apparent
that we are all caught in the throes of an educational revolution,
it is only too obvious that we are on shifting ground. Nowadays
more and more parents whose children are learning set theory,
say, or French in the primary school find themselves at a loss when
it comes to helping with homework. In many professional fields
candidates who have completed a course of studies and then delayed

taking their final examinations for a period of two or three years often find themselves at a serious disadvantage – so much has happened in the interim that the syllabus requirements are no longer the same. For their part, most self-respecting teachers find it increasingly difficult to keep abreast of all the latest developments and techniques; while married women, returning to the classroom after a decade or so, are apt to feel sadly out of touch.

The situation, indeed, is reminiscent of the one which existed in Athens just prior to the outbreak of the Peloponnesian War when, as Thucydides observes, citizens who had been abroad for only a few months found that the very meanings of words had altered during their absence. It is a time of cultural flux.

In view of the economic, political, and technological forces which combine to make this an age of rapid transition it would be very surprising if the outcome did not prove to be a social order (and with it an educational system) utterly unlike the one to which we are accustomed. If so, the question which should chiefly concern us is that of deciding [1] whether innovations in the schools are keeping pace with those affecting society at large, [2] whether these innovations are as well planned and as well co-ordinated as they need to be. It seems that on both counts the only possible answer is an emphatic NO.

At first blush, the Teaching Revolution may appear to involve nothing more than a wholesale extension of the use of audio-visual aids – pushbutton classrooms, language-laboratories, closed-circuit television, overhead projectors, concept films, programmed learning and all that – an extension which is still by no means widespread in the sense that many teachers either do not have these facilities or prefer to do without them.

There is, however, a second and much more interesting line of development which promises to bring about fundamental changes both in the subject-matter of what is taught as well as in its style of presentation. Such moves as the introduction of the New Mathematics and the shift of emphasis away from the printed page to the spoken word in the teaching of languages represent the first stirrings of a reform which is certainly as pregnant for the future as any electronic installation, say the computer-based teaching machine. The break-away from the formalism of traditional methods, first accomplished during the first half of the century in the realm of child art, is being followed in the second by kindred approaches in other school subjects, most notably of course in mathematics, physics, chemistry, and biology, but to an increasing extent also in English, modern languages, history, and even in religious instruction (where the impact of the 'new' theology is not without its own repercussions).

While it is not always clear just what these approaches have in common, apart from a vague dissatisfaction with the old ways of doing things, it is possible to discern the broad outlines of a new pedagogy. All begin with the determination to cut out the dead wood from the existing curriculum, to re-define the *content* of courses, to clarify its *structure*, and to specify the *objectives*. All insist on the importance of *sequence*, first in the careful ordering of the subject-matter itself, and second, in ensuring that the conceptual level of instruction is in keeping with the pupil's stage of development – in short, a combination of teacher – centred and child – centred approaches. Equally, all insist that wherever possible the learning situation should be kept open-ended – in other words, that the pupil should be trained in habits of self-directed inquiry and logical inference through being allowed to discover abstract principles for himself. Gone, one hopes for ever, is the abject notion that the art of teaching is nothing better than the process of imparting information, the philosophy of someone-who-knows-telling-those-who-don't. Gone, too, or going fast, is the age-old disposition to underrate the capacities of the average child and with it the readiness to write him off prematurely as non-academic. As we shall argue in the following chapter, the fuse which will assuredly spark off a genuine Teaching Revolution in our time is to be found in changes in the concept of educability which have only been brought to a head since mid-century, changes which have already produced a *volte-face* in official pronouncements as witnessed in the Crowther, Robbins, and Newsom Reports, and which demand fundamental rethinking on the part of administrators, teachers, and parents alike because they open up entirely new possibilities.

For the moment, however, it will be as well to agree that the revolution is, at best, prospective, and that its most obvious antecedents are: [1] the so-called new technologies of instruction, and [2] the revision of subject-matter and methods of teaching. In so far as both of these represent deliberate attempts to initiate changes in the schools, they may be thought of as comprising a number of discrete sub-movements, each of which tends to go its own way regardless of the others. For the sake of convenience, some of these sub-movements may be listed under the following headings:

A] *Organizational* – Team-Teaching
B] *Technological* – Programmed Learning
　　　　　　　　Closed-circuit Television
　　　　　　　　Language-Laboratories
C] *Curricular* – The New Mathematics
　　　　　　　The New Science
　　　　　　　The New English, etc.

What the bare list conceals, of course, is the wide range of disagreement which exists among the various groups of enthusiasts whose interests are largely identified with one or other of these sub-movements: for example, the rivalry between the Skinnerians and the Crowderians in the field of programmed learning, or the hostility between the advocates of 'free writing' and the 'new linguistics' school of thought in the teaching of English. Also concealed is the fact that at times some of these movements run counter to the others – for example, the small-step, fixed-sequence learning imposed by the typical linear programme seems, at any rate on the face of things, to be out of sympathy with the more intuitive, self-directed inquiry recommended by the leading spirits of the reform movement in other fields. Each coterie generates its own we-feelings, its own intellectual and emotional commitments and vested interests, to say nothing of its own jargon! Thus we find groups of teachers immersed in the problems of writing and testing programmed materials, others trying their hands at television, others preoccupied with a 'new' grammar, and so on and on and on – with the result that the reform movement as a whole is uneven in its advances, patchy in its coverage, and lacks any master-strategy. Worse still, it lacks an agreed, explicit theory of instruction which alone can guarantee its advance on a broad front. No one, apparently, feels able to take a synoptic view or to provide the overall rationale that is needed. Until such a rationale is forthcoming there is nothing for it but to resign ourselves to the prospect of endless muddling through, duplication of effort and abortive enterprises. Even if it seems presumptuous for any single individual to review the whole gamut of educational innovation and to try to elucidate its underlying *theoria*, *The Teaching Revolution* is written in the conviction that the attempt is worth making.

WANTED: A STRATEGY OF EDUCATIONAL REFORM

As one American critic puts it,

> The theorists of reform say little about how their visions of the new education can be realized, and the engineers of reform rarely have much to say about how the changes in instruction they are developing and testing will foster the realization of any basic educational goals. . . . Another major characteristic of the reform movement is the hasty, often superficial way in which the various innovations are being developed, implemented and evaluated. Most of the thousands of change programs under way in research centers or schools across the country suffer from the lack of adequate planning, adequate facilities, or adequate personnel.[1]

Ideally, the planning of any nation-wide education reform would allow for four more or less clearly defined stages: [1] a preliminary stage of controlled *experimentation* followed by [2] a stage of limited *implementation*, i.e. some kind of pilot-run leading to [3] a stage of final *evaluation* culminating in [4] a stage of universal *dissemination*. As it is, we find all four stages being run together simultaneously. Moreover, apart from a handful of research studies in the USA, precious little attention has been paid to the complex patterns and rates of change in educational systems, still less to its dynamics.* According to one such investigation, a whole century may elapse between the appearance of an innovation and its eventual diffusion throughout the entire system.[2] Prior to its appearance there is a kind of gestation period, marked by increasing turbulence and dissatisfaction, which lasts for about fifty years before giving birth to the new idea or invention. It takes another fifteen years before the latter finds its way into 3 per cent of the schools. Thereafter the rate of diffusion accelerates rapidly for approximately twenty years, by which time the innovation has come to be regarded as standard practice, except among the 'late developers' who require another fifteen years to bring acceptance up to 100 per cent.

Judging by the speed with which programmed learning, language-laboratories and other new developments have made their début, it seems that the rate of acceleration during the initial stage has increased fairly considerably in recent years – Mort's 3 per cent estimate was based on studies carried out in the 1930s – but the chances are that the process is still a good deal slower than the evangelists of reform like to think. One man's revolution is everyone else's nonsense during his lifetime, dangerous nonsense at that.

On the other hand, it is clear that concerted efforts can bring about wide-scale and dramatic transformations in theory and practice in a relatively short space of time: witness the successes of the School Mathematics Study Group in the USA, the impact already made by the Nuffield Science Project in England, and the virtually complete changeover to the Alternative Physics and Chemistry syllabuses in Scotland. Each of these ventures provides an interesting case-study, illustrating the logistic problems involved in mounting any major curricular reform.

Given a climate of opinion which is sufficiently critical of the old ways of doing things and sufficiently dissatisfied with their shortcomings to want them remedied, the task of re-defining

* The 'Resources for Learning' Project set up by the Nuffield Foundation is therefore timely. Initially it will collect information about innovations in method, etc, both from this country and from foreign educational systems. Its overall purpose is to investigate ways of improving the quality of the learning process in the 5–18 age range in English schools.

aims, content and lay-out is relatively easy. So, too, is the drafting of syllabuses. The real difficulties arise when it comes to feeding innovations into the mainstream of existing practice. If the efforts of the reformers are not to prove ineffectual, careful phasing and synchronization of the various moves is essential. Among these, the following may be listed, not necessarily in order of priority:

1] Writing, editing, approval, mass production and distribution of textbooks, apparatus, films, tapes, etc

2] Conducting a public relations campaign in order to gain the understanding and support of professional and public opinion

3] Arranging for joint consultation at all points with educational administrators, examining bodies, university entrance boards, etc

4] Organizing courses of in-service training for teachers

5] Re-organizing courses of pre-service training for teachers.

In the last resort, of course, the success of the operation depends upon [4] and [5], but it has to be borne in mind that faulty timing or failure to fulfil any single requirement – and there are others not listed here – can jeopardize the outcome. Revolutions do not come about by chance; they have to be schemed for, worked for and (when it comes to the crunch) fought for with all the intellectual acumen and passion that their instigators can muster.

Judged by its scope and vigour, today's educational reform movement may be reckoned impressive enough. The rate at which the production of mechanical gadgets of one sort or other is mounting may lull the unwary into supposing that a teaching revolution is on its way, as it were of its own accord. But to suppose that the lavish provision of classroom hardware will bring it in is as banal as to imagine that Utopia will arrive when every family possesses two cars. By British standards, the typical Texan school is designed as a *machine à enseigner*, equipped with all the latest mechanical aids, yet to a visitor many of the methods used seem almost old-fashioned. Obviously, we need to know a great deal more about patterns of change and the ways in which they are affected by patterns of culture. It is easy to talk glibly and in general terms about the impact of scientific technology (as we shall be doing in a moment!), and to forget that revolutions occur more frequently in backward, under-developed countries than they do in an affluent society. Necessity is the mother of invention, and it may well be that Britain's economic difficulties will provide the spur which has been lacking hitherto, just as the Sputnik scare did, for a time, in the USA. It may even be that the kind of pedagogy which we are groping towards has already been found in the poorer Communist-bloc countries and that ultimately our high-flown theorizing will reduce itself to the simplicity of Makarenko's axiom: 'If the pupil fails to learn the fault is in the teaching.' Certainly the first prerequisite for any grand strategy of educational reform is a viable theory of instruction.

In any case, the tremendous forces of resistance and inertia which have to be overcome cannot be minimized. Social scientists of all shades of opinion agree in thinking that, if only because its main concern is with the transmission of culture, the school must remain conservative. As the sociologist sees it, the school 'prepares children for change by encouraging permissive and critical attitudes, but it can only do this because they are already sufficiently accepted values of society. . . . It is a force which supports and develops the changes in social aims already decided by those in power, but it does not initiate the changes.'[3] Anthropologists, similarly, take a poor view of the chances of forward-thinking pressure-groups' making much headway against the powerful forces of tradition: in their judgement, the tail cannot wag the dog, and more than one promising reform movement – Progressive Education, for instance – has come to nought because it ignored this fact.[4]

Again, according to the system theorist, the school, like any other formal organization, has its own built-in regulatory processes which ensure maintenance of its stability.[5] To say this is not to exclude the possibility of sweeping changes occurring, simply to stress the point that the main source of change is to be sought *outside* the system of which the organization is a part, that the degree of change is directly proportional to the stimulus from the supra-system, and that the more hierarchical the internal structure of an organization is the more resistant it is likely to be to such stimulus. According to the system theorist's analysis, revolutionary upsets only occur when the stability of an organization is subjected to constantly increasing stress: what happens then is, first, a lag in response, followed by an overcompensatory response, and finally a catastrophic collapse.

Thus, to take an example of the kind of development that has been taking place in England since the 1944 Education Act, we find the adoption of a tripartite system of secondary schools gradually giving rise to public dissatisfaction and strongly voiced criticism of the selection procedures used in the 11-plus examination. So long as the dissatisfaction and the criticism did not rise to the level of an overwhelming protest the authorities remained on the defensive. The fairness of IQ tests, and their reliability as predictors of the child's suitability for this or that type of course were stoutly maintained: in short, the first reaction was a 'lag in response' and the upholding of the *status quo*. As the attacks persisted and gained in intensity, this somewhat intransigent attitude was gradually broken down, ending with a disavowal of the official policy and the adoption of the comprehensive principle. To recognize that the latter remains highly controversial is to acknowledge that many people regard it as an 'over-compensatory response'.

At this point, unfortunately for the neatness of the system theorist's analysis, an imminent collapse is usually averted, the stress lifted, and what follows tends to be in the nature of a compromise. All of which is a roundabout way of saying that the present indications are that the most we can reasonably look for is the accomplishment of far-reaching revisions, not a total recasting of the educational system. The auguries point to a steady amelioration rather than a violent overthrow of the old order.

Against this, we have to reckon with the external forces, not least those of technology, which induce their own stresses and exert their own pressures on the system.

THE IMPETUS FROM TECHNOLOGY

Trying to trace the origins of change, turns out to be a quest for the rainbow's end. It is an illusion to suppose that any single factor is responsible. Nevertheless, theorists as diverse in their interpretations as Marx, Veblen, Ogburn, Mumford, and Sumner agree in locating the *primum movens* of social change somewhere in the material culture – and in the twentieth century this means technology. In the past, as for example during the Renaissance and Reformation, *ideas* may seem to have been the mainspring and dynamic of cultural metamorphosis, but in the modern world there is little doubt that the emphasis is placed firmly on *things*. Granted, this is an oversimplification. In every age, the relationship between technics and culture needs to be thought of as being reciprocal, interactive. It may be, as Mumford argues, that human culture arose from primitive man's activities as a tool-making animal and that throughout the course of history technology, i.e. new ways of doing things, has always been and must always remain the real instigator and *vis a tergo* of progress. It may also be, as Ogburn's cultural-lag thesis holds, that the social discontinuities and maladjustments which characterize transition periods like the one through which we are now passing are due to unequal rates of change in the material and the non-material culture.

What cannot be denied is that it has become a truism to say that we live in an age that is dominated by scientific technology. 'In no other age have men lived with so dizzying a sense of change, or seen their basic material and social environment being made over, and made over again, so steadily. Technology, plainly, is the fundamental dynamic element in modern society.'[6] It affects a man's daily life from the moment he switches on his electric razor in the morning to the moment he tucks himself in beneath his electric blanket at night – and the equipment installed in the average kitchen nowadays is proof enough that it affects the housewife's way of life no less markedly. Technology is visibly changing the skyline of our cities and the landscape of our countryside, it is bringing about subtle changes within the family group, and dramatic changes in the nature and level of the work-skills that are necessary for the maintenance of an advanced industrial economy.

With new instruments of publication ready to hand the search for more effective systems of communication proceeds apace. Attempts to devise technologies of instruction – teaching machines, language-laboratories, closed-circuit television networks, etc – represent one step in that direction. In the circumstances, it is understandable that the authorities should look hopefully upon these ventures; understandable, too, that they should look upon technological innovation as a good thing.

The trouble is that the decision to go ahead with such experiments has to be taken in advance of any guarantee that the means will justify the end, and without any safe arbiter for appraising either their usefulness or their long-term effects. As yet, moreover, little or no attempt has been made to co-ordinate these developments with the result that each of them is left to go its own way, a point already noted; which means that there is a real danger that commercial enterprise may have more to do with their exploitation than any disinterested educational motives.

The speed with which programmed learning and the manufacture of self-instruction devices of one sort or other has developed since 1960 is one example of the invasive influence of technology in our schools. The provision of expensive switchgear installations like the language-laboratory is another. The pace-setting of Glasgow, Hull and other cities in the field of closed-circuit television is yet another.

The fact remains, nevertheless, that in all three cases the decision to go ahead has been taken more or less as an act of faith, that is, in the absence of any clear evidence that the results will be beneficial. To say this is not to criticize such ventures, simply to underline the fact that there must always be an element of uncertainty, even risk, in any decision which makes innovation possible.

At the same time it is worth asking whether we are nearing the situation in which 'things are in the saddle and ride men'. According to Toynbee's reading of history technical developments are largely independent of the civilization in which they take place: they have a continuity and durability which undercuts religious, moral, political, and social institutions alike – and which survives them. Thus, after the collapse of Hellenic civilization the techniques of iron-working, writing, and mathematics survived the cataclysm which befell the Ancient world and emerged unscathed to live on in the modern period. If this interpretation is correct, and it is certainly plausible, we are faced with a disconcerting possibility: that technological advance, if not actually continuous, is cumulative, whereas civilizations and cultures come and go seemingly without getting any forrader.

So far as the idea of human progress is concerned, this is a point of crucial significance. Can it be that the improvements in technology, which are there for all to see, have outstripped the improvability of man himself? Can it be that technology develops according to its own laws and that in the present state of our knowledge these laws are independent of any effective human control?

Such questions are far from being rhetorical. Even those thinkers who maintain that the relationship between technology and culture is always mutual, recognize that each and every invention is ambivalent, capable of good or evil according to the uses to which it is put. Thus Mumford, in a passage written more than thirty years ago, emphasises that all the time- and labour-saving devices which we have come to rely on – cars, telephones, radio, television, washing machines and the rest – *can* serve to enhance the individual's capacities for leading the good life:

> But there is a proviso attached to this promise, namely, that the culture of the personality shall parallel in refinement the refinement of the machine. . . . As with all instruments of multiplication, the critical question is as to the function and quality of what one is multiplying. There is no satisfactory answer to this on the basis of technics alone, certainly nothing to indicate, as the earlier exponents of instantaneous communication seem pretty uniformly to have thought, that the results will be automatically favorable to the community.[7]

There is further difficulty. Thanks to the age-old prejudice

in favour of 'liberal' studies and the disparagement of the applied
sciences our intellectual life suffers from a split personality. Both
inside and outside academic circles there are those who insist that
the aims of general education – variously defined as 'culture of
the personality', the 'nurture of personal growth', or 'the training
of the responsible human being and the citizen', can only be
achieved through the traditional disciplines of arts and pure
science. On the other hand, there are those who urge the need
for more work-based courses, for greater emphasis on practical as
distinct from theoretic studies, in short, for some kind of social
engineering.

There is, to be sure, a place for both. Pure science, it has been
remarked, makes things possible, but it is applied science that
gets things done.

On the whole, however, it has to be acknowledged that the
people who are in charge of the educational services – administrators, teachers, committee men – tend to belong to the first class.
Their background and outlook combine to make them unfamiliar
with, and sometimes unsympathetic towards, the reasoning of the
technocrats. In this situation, the latter's advice is either ignored, as
being beneath their notice, or it is taken on trust and followed
blindly.

The climate of opinion being what it is, the second of these
possibilities should give us pause no less than the first, for the
indiscriminate adoption of mechanical aids to teaching is likely
to prove as disastrous as their total rejection. As things are,
fashion decrees that in order to be 'with-it', an educational
authority, a school, or a teacher must acquire them, if only as status
symbols.

So one LEA orders a batch of loop-film projectors, regardless of
their limited usefulness (and maybe ignorant of their faulty design).
Another, not to be outdone, supplies a number of overhead
projectors and dumps them in classrooms where no one knows
how to handle them to the best advantage, if at all. Another votes
for language-laboratories and then leaves the teachers concerned
to find their own *modus operandi*, sometimes without the assistance

of a technician. More often than not it appears that the decision to purchase all this costly equipment owes more to a desire to keep up with the Joneses than to any more enlightened reason, and that high-pressure salesmanship has a good deal to do with it also.

Presumably the intention behind these package-deals is to save valuable time, to secure more efficient deployment of school staffs, to facilitate the learning process, and in the long run to economize in public expenditure. The truth is that in the short run, at any rate, none of these intentions looks like being achieved.

In the case of language teaching, for instance, we find some schools following BBC or ITA series, some taking a closed-circuit television course, some using language-laboratories, others trying out programmed texts, while the vast majority are left to carry on under more conventional methods. No doubt each of these latest adjuncts to teaching has its unique contribution to offer, but until it becomes clear what that contribution is there is bound to be duplication of effort, to say nothing of considerable wastage of time and money.

In some respects, too, it is evident that these new ventures occasionally find themselves at cross purposes with the established aims and methods of teaching in the schools. In the case of languages, including English, for example, the emphasis in all these so-called technologies of instruction is upon the spoken word, whereas the requirements of the leaving certificate examinations (themselves now in the process of being changed, of course) are still based on the pupil's understanding of print and the written word.

In any transitional stage it is, of course, inevitable that there should be some confusion, disagreement, and misunderstanding. In a sense, it is all to the good that local education authorities and individual schools and teachers should be left free to follow their own devices. In a sense, too, it is right and proper that the desire for final evaluation should be deferred so as not to interfere with the experimental work in hand.

Playing about with gadgets, unfortunately, all-too easily degenerates into messing about with them. Experimenting is one thing, tinkering quite another. What is needed, and at the highest level, is a national planning authority, an educational body akin to the *Délégation Générale à la Recherche Scientifique et Technique* in France. At the moment, not only is there no semblance of a High Command to give direction to policy, to finance major projects, and to provide joint consultation between educationists, administrators, economists, sociologists, and technologists, but the governmental attitude might well be characterized as one of *laissez-faire*. And if the bringing together of this team of all the talents is not within the bounds of practical politics, surely more could be done at local and regional levels to arrange for the thrashing-out of common problems between the various interested parties. In the first instance, something could be done right away to set up a working party to examine the pros and cons of mechanical classroom-aids and to assess the competing claims made for them. If it did nothing more, a broadly representative body including members of the teaching profession, the inspectorate, local authority officials, manufacturers of school equipment, publishers and others might help to rationalize the hit-or-miss, muddling-through approach which we have been content to follow so far. It might conceivably help to cut down to size some of the conspicuous consumption which (one cannot help suspecting) leads to the tax- and rate-payer's money being needlessly squandered.

Admittedly, the problem cannot be solved by calling conferences to discuss the human use of human inventions, neither does there seem much point in the devotees of 'liberal' education urging social engineers and the hardware merchants to be more mindful of their social responsibilities. But unless we are so defeatist as to relapse into the belief that technological progress really *is* uncontrollable, or so childish to accept its blessings as if they were toys dropped in our lap by some benevolent Father Christmas figure, we shall be left to drift, falling in with trends and tendencies as the whim takes us. In a word, we shall lack a policy.

THE EDUCATION EXPLOSION

Enough has been said to show that external pressures on the educational system have increased, are increasing and are certain to go on increasing. The impetus from technology alone has produced an inherent conflict between the school's traditional role, which was essentially conservative, and its responsibility to a society that demands adaptation to change.

The primary effect of all this on the school is to make mandatory continual changes in what is taught, even at fairly basic instructional levels. As computers have increased in complexity and usefulness, for example, changes in the elementary mathematics curriculum have become necessary in order that new members of society may be able to make more efficient use of the tools available to them. As our knowledge of the principles of physics, chemistry and biology expands, in both theoretical and practical terms, the content of secondary schools courses in these and other subjects must be altered to accommodate our new insights. Similarly, but at a different level, as new and increasingly specialized techniques and knowledge become necessary in many different blue-collar occupations, from the mechanical trades to agriculture, vocational training in these areas not only becomes more important but requires continual overhaul.[8]

Paradoxically, then, an argument which began by hinting that the school cannot be expected to figure as an agent of social change, except in a very limited way, ends with the assumption that it must provide the boldest lead. To ask why this should suddenly be thought necessary, remembering all the reasons that have been adduced against it in the past, is to suggest the answer.

The ability to innovate, to create a new art form or a new machine, or to produce a new solution to new problems in international affairs unquestionably requires a mastery of subject matter as well as a degree of intellectual discipline. But it also depends on a capacity for flexibility and the willingness to discard traditional techniques for approaching a problem. Particularly when the problems one is interested in solving are themselves changing rapidly and continually, not only in superficial content but also in formal structure. Assuming that our society and others throughout the world will continue to change at their current rates during the coming decades, we would argue that our present educational system must do more than provide students with a 'mastery of organized, systematic, and disciplined subject matter' if they are to be able to react in appropriate ways to the unique situations they will face as policy-makers and citizens of a world community in the twenty-first century. In fact, it appears likely that unless we take some major steps toward gearing our educational system to produce large numbers of highly sophisticated and flexible problem-solvers in the immediate future, we may not reach the twenty-first century, either as individuals or as a society.

The difficulty is that our capacity as a society for technological innovation has outstripped our ability to produce the *social* innovations necessary to accommodate either our changing technology or the changes wrought by our advancing technical skills.[9]

The cogency of all this can hardly be denied. Indeed, in order to understand what is happening, and what is almost certainly going to happen in the foreseeable future, it is necessary to review current developments in educational theory and practice within the context of the Education Explosion. The latter, unlike the Teaching Revolution (which it necessitates), cannot be accused of being a bravado term. It stands for the phenomenal and relentless increase in the demands now being made on the educational services at all levels and in all countries; and it has three interrelated aspects: [1] the explosion of numbers, [2] the explosion of information, and [3] the explosion of human aspirations and expectations.

THE EXPLOSION OF NUMBERS

That there is a population boom goes without saying. Between 1850 and 1950 the world population rose from 1,100 million to 2,500 million and is confidently expected to follow a steepening growth-curve which will bring it to 6,000 million by the end of the century. The population of Mexico doubled between 1930 and 1960 – to cite an isolated case. According to reliable estimates there will be at least three-quarters of a million *extra* pupils entering British primary schools in 1970. The effects of successive tidal waves in the birth-rate – first the 'Bulge', then the 'Trend' – are only too familiar. Overcrowded schools, oversized classes, and a chronic shortage of teachers are only some of the more obvious ones. They account, as much as any other single factor, for the public's growing concern about the quality and the quantity of the educational provision.

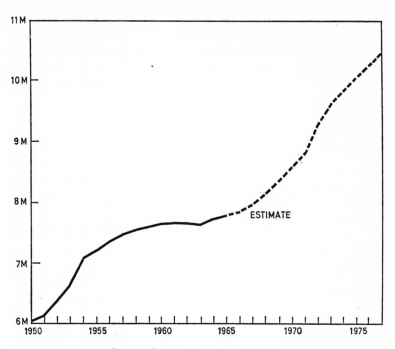

FIG I   Increase in the numbers attending school in England and Wales, 1950–1977. (The total school population numbered 6 millions in 1930 and 5.59 millions in 1938)

The annual rate of increase, which varies from 0·4 per cent in Western Europe, to 3–4 per cent in parts of Asia and South America, shows no signs of levelling off, and although eventually some kind of saturation point may be anticipated, the upward trend must be expected to continue more or less indefinitely. Moreover, so far as the underdeveloped countries are concerned the chief factor is not so much an increase in the birth-rate itself as a sharp reduction in the death-rate. Thanks to improved medical care, higher standards of living (*and* rising standards of education) more people than ever before now enjoy a much longer expectation of life. This, in turn, affects the composition of the various age-groups in society: for example, the proportion of old-age pensioners in Britain is going to increase very considerably during the next twenty years. Another factor which has to be borne in mind is the secular trend towards earlier maturity: physically, at least, children are growing up faster than they used to in previous generations. Yet another stems from the nature of industrial society which requires that the numbers needing an extended school-life – 'further education' as it is quaintly called – be steadily increased. No matter where the spotlight of attention is turned – on the primary, secondary, or tertiary stages of the continuous process – it is the same story everywhere. 'The horde is out there craving for admission.' In terms of human arithmetic, the pressure is on and no mistake.

THE EXPLOSION OF INFORMATION

These demographic trends coincide with, and are made possible by, the extraordinary advance of knowledge in every field, more particularly in the applied sciences. During the first Industrial Revolution the division of labour necessary for mass production was satisfied by an educational system which catered for an intellectual élite while providing the bare minima of literacy and numeracy for 'a multitude of laborious poor'. The requirements of the second Industrial Revolution (Mumford's neo-technic phase) are more exacting, presupposing much higher standards of proficiency as well as greater adaptability on the part of the many as well as of the few.

As the Long Revolution gathered momentum the pace of technological and cultural change alike accelerated, which explains why curricula and methods of teaching which took a hundred years or more to become established now find themselves faced with the prospect of dissolution within a decade or less. Being commonplace, their soundness has come to be so taken for granted that it is only natural that most teachers should wish to see them preserved intact as having stood the test of time. But appeals to Time Past are of no avail: conventional practice already falls short of the demands imposed by an insistent present and cannot hope to meet the yet greater demands of an imminent future.

In most fields of inquiry the build-up of information is taking place so quickly that subject-matter which was formerly thought essential now has to be discarded as so much lumber. It is easy to exaggerate, of course. Cynics may say that what we have to do with in the field of educational studies, at any rate, is not so much an explosion of information as an explosion of words; and that books sired by the spirit of publish-or-be-damned have added little to the sum of human knowledge, and nothing at all in the way of wisdom.

A sad commentary on our efforts, perhaps, but even if it were true it would do nothing to ease the heavy burden of 'required reading' which all must carry. It is the penalty of being born in the twentieth century, and year by year it becomes more harassing. As late as Victorian times it was still possible to think of the university as a collection of books, as if the sum of human knowledge could comfortably be housed in a library. Today, with so much more to be learned by so many, the educationist is forced to resort to other media and is more inclined to think in terms of a University of the Air.

The Explosion of Information is also an explosion of information *about* information. Industrialists and business men are not the only ones who must look to computer technology to solve their problems of information storage, retrieval, and display. It has been said that any tenable learning theory must, in the long run, be a branch of information theory, and the same is probably true of any viable theory of instruction also. Educationists who have watched the bibliography of programmed learning and auto-instruction grow prodigiously in recent years may be forgiven if they feel that this latest demand on their know-how is the last straw. Unfortunately, there is no escaping it.

Clearly, the kind of teaching which was appropriate to an age of coal and steam is no longer in keeping with an age of electronics.

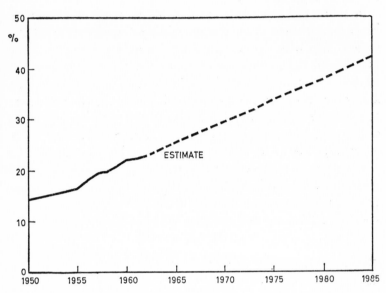

FIG 2 Percentage of pupils aged sixteen or over remaining at school (England and Wales) 1950–1985

Not only that, but if the projections of the economist agree with those of the sociologist we must anticipate a decline in the number of semi-skilled occupations and a steady rise in the level of qualifications of the mass of workers. In every walk of life, the need for expertise is imperative. Whether we call it knowledge or know-how, the mastery of enormous amounts of information is indispensable.

In the past most of this essential information was transmitted vertically, i.e. from parents, teachers, and other adults to the young; and because its content remained more or less the same from one

c

generation to the next, its inputs were largely contained within an institutional framework, i.e. schools and colleges, specially designed for that purpose. Nowadays, by comparison, the output of new information is so vast that much of it is being simultaneously transmitted by agencies outside the formal educational system – the mass media, for example.

In short, the indications are that the shortage of teachers is likely to be permanent and that the existing educational institutions cannot cope with the ever-growing demands made upon them. New systems of communication are evidently required. Attempts to devise modern technologies of instruction, inadequate as they are, are prompted by the urgency of the need. One way or other, the teacher's productivity (meaning his power to mediate ideas, skills, experiences, and information more widely and more effectively) has to be stepped up as never before. Failing this, the pressure of numbers and the pressure of demand for higher standards will, between them, precipitate the kind of collapse predicted by the system theorist. It is a race against time. Either we have a Teaching Revolution or we must expect a shambles.

THE EXPLOSION OF HUMAN ASPIRATIONS AND EXPECTATIONS

In the Educated Society, we are told, only the qualified man achieves status: in Whitehead's parlance, he must know something well and be able to do something well, otherwise he stands a good chance of being unemployable. In an advanced industrial society the demand for higher standards of paper qualifications is inexorable, which explains why specialist courses proliferate as they do. Moreover, the demand creates its own supply, i.e. socio-economic pressures conspire to make more and more people acquire the information and skills which will enable them to find their places in a meritocracy. 'The cat is out of the bag. The simple equation Education equals Power has suddenly been grasped by the masses the world over.'[10]

But the problem of communication does not stop short at the

dissemination of information and skills. Even more acute is the problem of catering for adaptability, including the right use of leisure. Work-based courses are all very fine, but what is to happen in an age of full automation if work itself becomes largely redundant?

The exploitation of mechanical aids to efficient learning has, as yet, done little to alleviate the problem of general education, the kind of education which 'appeals deeply to each and yet remains in goal and essential teaching the same for all'. For that matter, it is not immediately obvious how or whether it can so long as the learner's motivation remains unchanged.

Ironically, the tension between the general and the special aim springs from an ambivalence in human nature itself. In modern industrial societies this tension becomes aggravated into an open conflict in which the motives for wanting more and better educa- tion are seen to be engaged in a perpetual tug of war. On the one hand, both the state and the individual look upon education as an *investment* and expect handsome dividends for the time, effort, and money expended upon it. For most people, equality of oppor- tunity means opportunity to 'get on in life', and the only royal road for those who aspire to become leaders in the rat race is the one which leads via the 11-plus examination to O- and A-levels and thence to some form of professional training. On the other hand, education is desired for its own sake, for the intrinsic worth of a culture which exemplifies 'the best that has been thought and said in the world', in a word, as *consumption*.

Now the three progressive stages as envisaged in the 1944 Education Act reflect three parallel stages in the social history of the British people. The first stage dates from the onset of the Industrial Revolution. It took the whole of the nineteenth century to provide free elementary schooling for all, the ground floor of a national system which is still not complete. Even in the poverty- stricken conditions of the Bleak Age there was always the Oliver Twist who dared to ask for more, and as the nineteenth century drew to its close the demand from parents who had themselves received only an elementary education grew more vociferous.

Accordingly, 'Free Secondary Education for All' became the war-cry of the early decades of the twentieth century. In an attempt to satisfy the popular demand, successive plans for erecting a second storey to the existing structure were put forward between 1926 and 1944, culminating in the tripartite arrangement recommended by the Norwood Report.

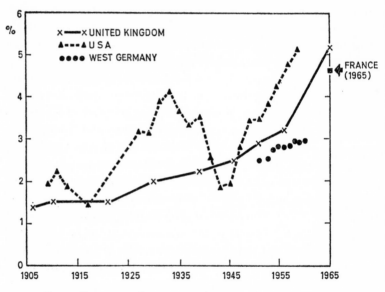

FIG 3 Expenditure on education in the United Kingdom 1905–1965 as a percentage of the Gross National Product. (Percentages for West Germany (1950–1960) and the United States (1909–1959) are from *The Economics of Education*, edited by E. A. G. Robinson and J. E. Vaizey, Macmillan, 1966)

Culminating? The present controversy raging over the comprehensive school is proof enough that a fully satisfactory arrangement has yet to be worked out, and that the evolution of the secondary stage is by no means completed. Even so, its aftermath can already be seen in the rapid increase in the numbers of 'first-generation' students at the universities. More and more parents who attended grammar schools and left before reaching the sixth form now expect their children to stay on and aim at some kind of degree award. Many who previously were reluctant to encourage their children to do this because of the financial hardships and the loss of earnings entailed by a protracted course of study now feel that they have no cause for worry. With career prospects in mind, it is no longer a question of whether they can afford it, but rather one of deciding whether their children's future status will be impaired if they are not allowed to proceed to some form of higher education. In the same way that elementary schooling for all gradually led to secondary schooling for all, so now we are in the throes of an upward extension of the educational ladder and must anticipate developments at the tertiary stage comparable with those which have already taken place in the two lower stages.

The signs are that the construction of this upper storey of the national system will be completed fairly rapidly. Colleges of advanced technology, first designated after the 1956 White Paper have emerged as fully-fledged technological universities within the space of a decade. Two-year training colleges, also in the ascendant, now find their style enhanced as colleges of education and offer their own B.Ed. degrees. New universities have sprung up all over the country and plans for others continue to be mooted despite the temporary embargo on additional new foundations. Extra-mural courses are multiplying as fast as they can be organized. Soon the technical colleges and colleges of further education will be vying for recognition alongside the other institutions of higher education. The line of demarcation between 'higher' and 'further' is becoming blurred.

The mushrooming of the sixth form in the English grammar school (the percentage of seventeen-year-olds in attendance rose from 7·9 to 12 between 1954 and 1962), is only one isolated, insular example of a world-wide trend. Fears that expansionist programmes to meet the growing pressure of demand for university places might result in an all-round lowering of standards, that 'more means worse', have not been realized and are not likely to be. On the contrary, all the available evidence shows that standards rise as the educational base is widened. Any suggestion that popularization necessarily means vulgarization must be firmly rejected. More so than any other single factor, élitist thinking wedded to the notion of a limited pool of ability has been responsible for holding back progress and for keeping the provision of education in Britain pegged at an unnecessarily modest level.

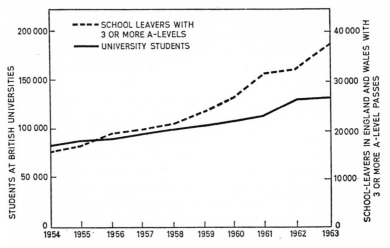

FIG 4　Students at British universities and school-leavers with three or more passes at A-level (England and Wales) 1954-1963

Quite apart from other considerations, the 'pool' has increased for a demographic reason, as Mr H. L. Elvin points out:

The number of eighteen-year-olds in Great Britain in 1955 was 642,000. The number in 1965 is 963,000. This, of course, reflects the jump in the number of births after the last war, but it shows that the demand by qualified students for higher education in 1965 was bound to be greater, *from this cause alone*, than it was in 1955, and without any lowering of standards.[11]

But the cause is not solely a demographic one. What has to be reckoned with is a growing disposition on the part of the mass of ordinary people to think more highly of themselves, to want to make more of themselves, to be more critical of the shortcomings of the education they have received. Along with this, however dimly, goes the conviction that the resources of the welfare state ought to be used to make good their shortcomings. The time is past when they could be fobbed off with second-bests. 'More means better' is coming to be their slogan. What is more, they have the support of psychologists and sociologists whose findings point irresistibly to the conclusion that many of the accepted beliefs about the educability of the masses are in need of sharp revision.

SOCIAL CLASS INFLUENCES

It is easy to see why in recent years so many official reports and research investigations have been obsessed with the influence of social class. No accident, either, that the findings have received so much publicity.

15–18, Half Our Future, Higher Education, one by one, the areas of neglect in the English system of education have been exposed, and with them the extent to which the nation's reservoir of talent remains untapped. A whole series of local and regional surveys, among others those reported by Floud, Halsey, and Martin in Middlesbrough and S. W. Herts, by Dr Barron Mays in the Crown Street district of Liverpool and by Jackson and Marsden in the West Riding of Yorkshire, has disclosed the existence of an 'interlocking network of inequalities' in the system. It is now realized that this operates as a kind of underground passive resistance so as to render the legal provision of equal opportunity, if not a mockery, less effectual than was generally supposed at the time of the passing of the 1944 Education Act.

Full employment and fatter pay-packets, it appears, have done nothing to make large sections of the working class (particularly those engaged in unskilled and semi-skilled occupations) feel disposed to take full advantage of the educational services available to them. So far as the grammar school and the university are concerned, these people are virtually non-starters. It is as though they had opted out of the system. These disincentives to learning and the resulting under-achievement are clearly delineated in the facts and figures relating to the 'Robinson' children in the Newsom Report. These are the 'problem children' who come from 'problem areas', the ones who refuse to wear school uniform, who tend to play truant, who do not want to do homework, who leave at the earliest opportunity, who in short seem to want no part of what the school has to offer. Significantly, these children also tend to be undersized and underweight.

Vastly more research will have to be done before the plight of these unfortunates can be alleviated. For the under-achievement of the 'Robinson' boys and girls is not to be remedied simply by moving their families into new housing schemes, and accommodating them in up-to-date school buildings – though in the first instance improved physical conditions are, of course, essential. Their failure to respond has much deeper causes, however. It is the nature of these pre-dispositions to learning that we need to know more about.

One of these concerns the mode of speech peculiar to the sub-culture. In a typical lower working-class family a syntactically simple language prevails (Bernstein's 'restricted code'). Its most limiting characteristic is an avoidance of the expression of abstract ideas: more often than not, words fail when it comes to the deeper meanings, which are conveyed by gesture. Because of this, the level of conceptualization remains low. The gap between this primitive vernacular and the more sophisticated language in common usage in the middle classes (Bernstein's 'elaborated code') creates a sense of dislocation in the minds of many pupils from lower working-class backgrounds. In turn, the dislocation between the kind of language they are familiar with at home and the one they are expected to conform with in the classroom, leads to alienation. Everything about the school – its ethos, its regulations, its rewards and punishments – makes them ill at ease. Very often they find themselves in what can only be called a persecutory learning situation. The upshot is that many of them decide at an early stage that they are 'not clever'. The value system to which the school is geared is strangely unlike the one they are pledged to in the sub-culture. They do not belong. Their aspirations and expectations lie elsewhere. And the trouble is that the limitations imposed by the language of the sub-culture cannot be removed by lessons on 'correct' grammar and speech-training.

No less incorrigible is the improvidence which characterizes the working-class's philosophy. This attitude of mind is dominated by a fatalistic belief in blind chance. Of all the pre-disposing factors which are antipathetic to school-bound learning this is the one which is likely to prove most intractable. It is, in the words of an eminent psychologist,

> an attitude towards life that is governed by the concept of luck. This means that there is really nothing you can do by your own efforts, that things happen to a considerable extent by luck. The business of applying the mind, the idea that man has a chance if he will use his mind, is an attitude which is not frequently present and which has to be created. This is an extremely difficult thing to do and I hope no one asks me how you do it, because I do not know.

A luck-dominated culture looks to the Pools and the Bingo Palace for its rewards, not to the school. As regards the latter, its verdict is summed up by the Marburton youth's terse comment, 'Christ, what a bloody way of growing up!'

If the picture presented is depressing it is because the condition of the lower orders, as they used to be called, has been depressed by circumstances. To lay all the blame at the doors of the school would be unfair, but no one who has studied the formative period of the English system of education will be left in any doubt about the historical determinants. Looking back, it is tempting to say that the masses have been conditioned to a numb acceptance of their lot: almost as if by design, the effect of the teaching to which they have been subjected has been to induce an inferiority complex. The institutionalizing of failure has been rationalized and made into a fine art in the selection procedures of English education. Small wonder we are left with so many rejectees.

As the evidence presented by the sociologists accumulates a radical change of outlook is discernible both in the field of educational theory and that of policy-making. To begin with, social class influences were seen simply as barriers to opportunity, but as the investigations proceeded their significance came to be seen in a total cultural perspective. As Mrs Floud explains:

> In so far as social class was seen to influence educational *performance* the problem was conceived of as a material one: how to mitigate the handicaps of poverty, malnutrition and over-crowding by using the schools as social agencies – by distributing free milk and meals to necessitous children and developing the school medical services. Only in the post-war period has the continuing attempt to democratize secondary and higher education in unfamiliar conditions of full employment and widespread prosperity confronted as with the need to formulate the problem more subtly and to see social class as as a profound influence on the *educability* of children.[12]

For the educationist, therefore, it is an age of great expectations. Unfortunately, in the absence of a viable theory of instruction, it is not at all clear how he can live up to them. Catering for the special aim, i.e. extending the range and availability of professional training in all its forms, is difficult enough as it is. But this pre-occupation with investment policies does nothing to solve the problem of general education (consumption), and to the extent that it is concerned with means rather than ends may be thought to aggravate it. It may be that Sir Eric Ashby is right in saying that, for some, the way to culture in the modern world is through a man's specialism, but does this hold good for all? The dangers of an homogenized, fatuous culture are only too apparent, as are the ways in which the mass media batten upon them. For the first time in history, millions of semi-educated men and women find themselves at a loose end, not knowing what to do with themselves, ready prey for the show-biz merchants and the not-so-hidden persuaders.

Empty minds? Empty lives? It would be treasonable to the cause of democracy to think so. As one educationist puts it:

> The conscious and unconscious enemies of democracy sometimes cite the results of the testing movement to support the thesis that

ordinary men and women are incapable of participating intelligently in the direction of public affairs. Basically, the notion that intelligence test data demonstrate the incapacity of the common man rests upon confusion and misunderstanding: confusion in the use of the word intelligence and misunderstanding of the meaning of intelligence test scores. Fundamentally, the term intelligence means the ability to understand and deal effectively with practical situations and problems; and it is in this sense that the intelligence of the common man is significantly related to his capacity to share in the direction of public affairs. Obviously, intelligence so defined is in part a function of learning and experience; hence, competence can usually be improved by education and training. And in any case, intelligence tests are designed to measure a certain type of learning capacity. Hence, the argument is sometimes made that the results of these tests show that the ordinary man is fatally deficient in the capacity to learn. But here again the argument is based upon misunderstanding and misinterpretation. In the first place, intelligence tests do not ordinarily measure learning capacity in general but only a particular type of learning ability – that involving the use of abstract symbols. In the second place, it is now definitely established that the scores on these tests are influenced by environmental opportunity, only the degree of which remains at issue. And even with respect to degree, while some investigations are still open to question, it is clear that under certain circumstances, such as poverty-stricken environment in the formative years the degree of environmental influence may be high.[13]

To which, by way of reinforcing the argument he adds:

Moreover, it should be noted that even the empirical demonstration that persons of a particular IQ cannot be taught certain things by the methods now employed proves nothing whatever about their capacity to learn these same things when and if better methods are employed (especially methods that relate abstract, verbal principles to the concrete situations to which they apply).[14]

In similar vein, the writer goes on to berate those critics who complain about the lack of interest and the low levels of taste by ordinary people in aesthetic affairs. To blame this on an assumed stupidity of the masses, he argues, is to overlook the fact that in literature, music, painting, the modern artist addresses himself in the first instance not to a public audience, but to a select coterie and in terms so esoteric as to be meaningful only to the initiated.

The conclusion to which we are driven is that if the social behaviour of many adults strikes us as being crass and inept there must have been something crass and inept in their upbringing. These people are indeed the victims of a 'poverty-stricken environment in their formative years'.

On all sides there are heartening signs that as the provision of education rises above the least common denominator level so the level of 'low culture' begins to merge into 'high culture'. There is today an upsurge in all forms of popular self-expression, from do-it-yourself outfits to art classes, amateur dramatics, choral and orchestral societies, model-making, gardening clubs, discussion groups, adult education classes and a host of others. This yearning for a fuller, richer life may have arisen from higher standards of formal education and from high standards of living yet it transcends them. It is the yeast beneath the surface ferment of our time.

> For the revolution of modernity has not only been a material revolution or an intellectual revolution. It has been a moral revolution of extraordinary scope, a radical alteration in what the human imagination is prepared to envisage and demand. And it has changed the dimensions in which we measure happiness and unhappiness, success and failure. It has given us the sense that we can make our own history; it has led us to impose new and more exacting demands on ourselves and our leaders; it has set loose the restless vision of a world in which men might be liberated from age-old burdens, and come to set their own standards and govern their own lives. . . .
>
> The revolution of modernity proposed to put men squarely on Prometheus' side. It is a unique venture in human affairs, and we can only relieve the strains and tensions it has created by taking it seriously. Our disappointments are real. But they are real because our powers are great and our expectations legitimately high.[15]

Too grandiose a manifesto? Perhaps it is. But if educational practice is to match the high hopes of Everyman dare educational theory set its sights any lower? To do that would be an inexcusable failure of nerve. Short of denying that the aspirations and expectations engendered by the Education Explosion are well-founded and legitimate, the inference is clear: as teachers we have our marching orders.

REFERENCES

1 Glenn Heathers 'Team Teaching and The Educational Reform Movement', pp. 345–6 in *Team Teaching*, ed. Chaplin and Olds, Harper Row, 1964

2 Paul R. Mort 'Studies in Educational Innovations from the Institute of Administrative Research: An Overview', *Innovation in Education*, p. 317, ed. M. B. Miles, Teachers College, Columbia University Bureau of Publications, 1964

3 A. K. C. Ottoway *Education and Society*, p. 12 and p. 56, Routledge and Kegan Paul, 1953

4 Cf. G. F. Kneller *Educational Anthropology*, pp. 90 et seq., Wiley, 1965

5 Daniel E. Griffiths 'Administrative Theory and Change in Organizations', *Innovation and Education*, pp. 425 et seq. (*v. supra*)

6 Charles Frankel *The Case for Modern Man*, pp. 197–8, Harper & Row, 1956

7 L. Mumford *Technics and Civilization*, Routledge, 1934

8 David A. Goslin *The School in Contemporary Society*, p. 45, Scott, Foresman, 1965

9 Ibid., p. 87

10 Marjorie Reeves (ed.) *The Problem of 18 Plus*, Introduction, Faber, 1965

11 H. L. Elvin *Education and Contemporary Society*, p. 60, Watts, 1965

12 Quoted by H. L. Elvin, op. cit., pp. 46–47

13 W. O. Stanley *Education and Social Integration*, p. 155, Teachers College, Columbia University, 1953

14 Ibid., p. 157

15 Charles Frankel *The Case for Modern Man*, pp. 208–9, Harper & Row, 1956

CHAPTER TWO

The Changing Concept of Educability

That education is the art of the possible has always been a trite saying. It implies that both the theory and practice of teaching are hedged about with so many ifs and buts that it is unrealistic to expect them to make silk purses out of sow's ears. Within the last ten years, however, the limits of the possible have suddenly been extended. Dramatic advances in a number of fields – in psychology, sociology, neurology, genetics, linguistics, above all in the technology of communication – necessitate a fundamental re-thinking of the concept of human educability. It is no longer a question of whether or not feats of learning which were once thought to be out of the question are within the reach of the average child. Ways and means of teaching him to read at the age of three, using a 'talking typewriter', or at a later stage of training him in reflective thinking with a machine endowed with artificial intelligence, are now available. We may not like them, but at least we cannot blink the fact that they exist. That tiresome truism is due for revision: education is the art of the seemingly impossible.

For the teacher who is *nel mezzo del cammin di nostra vita* this calls for a new appraisal which is certain to prove as uncomfortable as it is difficult. Shedding one's stock notions is never easy, but the situation demands it. The blinkers are off and he must raise his sights.

'We begin with the hypothesis that any subject can be taught effectively in some intellectually honest form to any child at any stage of development. It is a bold hypothesis and an essential one in thinking about the nature of the curriculum. No evidence exists to contradict it; considerable evidence is being amassed that supports it.'[1]

As a first tenet of faith, this is at once arresting and charged with profound significance, expressing as it does the buoyant mood of educational theory in the second half of the twentieth century. Yet the concept of educability it offers is by no means entirely novel. Its pedigree can be traced back to the French *philosophes*, and beyond them to the guiding spirits of the Reformation, in particular, the Comenian ideal of teaching all things to all men. Again, the concept bears a striking resemblance to that envisaged by radical thinkers like Francis Place, James Mill, and Robert Owen during the early decades of the nineteenth century, a view summed up in the assertion that, 'the generality of children are so organized as to be pretty nearly alike and may, by proper management, be made pretty nearly equally virtuous and wise'; only now, instead of being made to look ridiculous by the social context of the Victorians, the concept can be stated almost as if its truth were self-evident. So long as rigid social-class distinctions served to keep people in their proper stations, and so long as deterministic theories about the nature and distribution of human abilities remained unchallenged it was, of course, inevitable that the Utilitarians' assertion that 'Any man may learn any thing, one person as well as another', should seem to fly in the face of good sense, for it was only too evident that the 'proper management' on which the plausibility of the assertion depended had yet to be discovered.

Accordingly, throughout the nineteenth and early twentieth centuries British schools were organized on the principle that only a minority of pupils could be classified as academic, the rest as non-academic and that there was nothing for it but to assign them to different types of course. Moreover, it was generally assumed that certain subjects – foreign languages, geometry, algebra, physics and others – were so abstruse as to rule out any possibility of their being introduced to all pupils at the primary stage.

Now, suddenly, we are informed that a very different persuasion is needed. According to this hypothesis, undreamed-of possibilities are opened up by the methodologists and the shapers of the new curricula; and while it may be true that the vast majority of teachers still cannot bring themselves to agree that 'no evidence exists to contradict it', there is undoubtedly a growing disposition to question received opinions about the limits of educability and a growing conviction that the abilities of the average child have been grossly underestimated in the past. With the Pool of Ability myth exposed as a deceptive half-truth, a new dimension has been added to our educational thought. For theorist and for practitioner alike there is a ferment stirring in the mind, a ferment that has so far eluded every attempt to set it in order. After its long winter of discontent, educational theory finds itself caught between two worlds of discourse, one of which is not yet dead, the other powerless to be born: midway it seems, between a largely discredited cult of IQ and the worship of an unknown god called Creativity.

Here, indeed, is a word to conjure with, as full of promise (and as defiant of exact definition) as *Anshauung* was in Pestalozzi's day or *Darstellung* in Froebel's. Abracadabra or shibboleth? Whatever it means – and its very uncertainty is the measure of its potential significance – it is the kind of word which is nicely calculated to arouse a wild surmise. Liam Hudson observes wryly that it 'covers everything from the answers to a particular kind of psychological test to forming a good relationship with one's wife'.[2]

In Kneller's judgement,

In our time the study of creativity exercises a growing fascination. One reason is that it forms one of those rare meeting grounds of science and art that give practitioners heady glimpses of each other's business. Another is the very elusiveness of the creative process, which intrigues the inquiring mind, permitting it more than usual freedom to speculate.

But the main reason is that today more than ever we are realizing the need to educate in depth. Now that we have built up a considerable body of knowledge about human behavior, of which creativity

D

is a unique and invaluable aspect, education no longer can restrict itself to rote learning. Informed people insist that educators of all types add a third dimension to their task, that of cultivating human creativity in its finest sense.[3]

And yet, and yet . . . 'I hate books! They only tell us about things we know nothing about'. The force of Rousseau's paradox is brought home to the reader of most of the studies of creativity which have been published in recent years. One is reminded, too, of the oft-voiced complaint of the 'Creative English' enthusiasts – that teachers who are keenest on grammar invariably write the dullest of dull prose styles, if they write anything at all; for the fact is that the systematic investigation of the mysteries of the creative impulse and the creative act is normally carried out by the kind of people who are not themselves creative in any meaningful sense.

When it comes to deciding what that meaningful sense is to be it is necessary to obey Wittgenstein's injunction and remind ourselves of the word games with which this fuzziest of educational terms, 'creativity', has come to be associated.

The first point to be noted is that the word's usage, if not its derivation, is American in origin.* 'Inventiveness', 'originality', 'talent', 'imagination', 'giftedness', 'aptitude', 'special ability', 'genius', 'the exceptional child' – each and all of these carry kindred meanings and share a family resemblance in current English usage. As a generic term, 'creativity' is more comprehensive in its implications. The essential difference between the two usages – English – English and American–English – is best brought out by remarking that the former implies that in all its guises the creative attribute must be considered to be extremely rare, the exception rather than the rule. The latter is nothing like so restrictive.

The second point to be noted is that the usage of the term, and the considerable literature which has sprung up around it, is

* As a matter of interest, when the author used the word in the manuscript of a previous book its existence was queried by the publisher's editorial staff and subsequently by the printer's galley-proof reader!

quite recent. Prior to 1950, only 186 research studies out of the 121,000 titles listed in the *US Index of Psychological Abstracts* dealt with this problem. In Britain interest in it was first aroused, if not actually brought to a head after the publication of Getzels and Jackson's *Creativity and Intelligence* in 1962. The reasons for this sudden preoccupation on the part of psychologists and educationists are complex, a blend of purely disinterested motives and social, political, and economic influences. Thanks to this, the concept is no longer confined to the role of the artistic genius. Instead, the talk nowadays is of the creative scientist, the creative business man, even the creative military leader. There is, as Bruner observes, a shrillness to our contemporary concern with creativity, and there is certainly force in his comment that, 'The road to banality is paved with creative intentions'. In its New World setting, indeed, the drive for creativity may be construed as nothing better than a revised version of go-getting, advertising itself with such slogans as 'Increase your idea power' where formerly it was content to lure the half-educated with 'Increase your word power'. To what base uses it may lead the unwary should give us pause. What, for example, is one to make of courses in 'Creativized (*sic*) Electrical Engineering' – or, for that matter, of so-called brain-storming sessions in which anything goes and the participants deliberately set aside criticism and commonsense in the name of an alleged 'Principle of Deferred Judgement'? Surely, the fundamental error in ventures of this sort is to consider creativity merely as a kind of problem-solving; for the desire to exploit it for utilitarian purposes (as if it were a technique in the training of efficiency experts) can lead only to the worst of sophistries. For 'creativity' read 'productivity' and the shallowness of such advocacy is revealed for what it is worth.

There is, indeed, a brash egalitarianism about some of these pronouncements which needs to be treated with caution. From this viewpoint, as Kneller puts it, 'the psychological processes of James Joyce writing *Finnegan's Wake* do not differ fundamentally from those of an electrician deciding how best to wire a redecorated room',[3] a proposition which invites, and merits, the scorn of the literary critic if of no one else. Yet this egalitarianism is symptomatic of the explosion of aspirations and expectations which has been brought about by rising standards of mass education. While this may not have gone so far as to foster the widespread impression that 'You, too, can be a Van Gogh', it has seemingly bred a climate of opinion in which the individual feels that he has latent capabilities that can and ought to be brought out and developed. All that is needed to trigger off a genuine education explosion, and with it a truly dramatic teaching revolution, is to demonstrate that the average person's dimly held conviction that he is capable of better things is fully justified. The inherent promise of current investigations in the field of creativity is that they will provide such a demonstration. It is perfectly true that the term embraces a whole gamut of meanings (another way of saying that it covers a multitude of sins,), and that, as yet, precious little is certainly known about it. At the same time, a fair summary of the present findings is that:

> Though we have barely begun to explore these implications we know that they go to the heart of our teaching methods, the textbooks we use, the ways in which we design school curricula and so on. We know now that creativeness is not only the art teacher's business; it is everybody's business. We really only have scratched the surface; but we have made enough of a scratch to know that a whole new world of human potential lies underneath.[4]

Before going on, it is worth saying that the first breakthrough in this sector came in the early years of the century with the discovery of child art. It was the insights of such pioneers as Cizek and Viola which first highlighted the arguments in favour of a teaching method that turned its back on the fussy formalism of the art schools and preferred, instead, to place its trust in the learner's self-activity. 'Give them the tools and they will finish the job', was its motto. The results, as all the world knows, speak for themselves. Behind the loose talk about 'free expression', 'self expression' and all that there was the intuitive recognition that the learning situation ought to be, as we now say, open-ended; that traditional methods, particularly those based on the Herbartian model, were too narrowly restrictive, relying too heavily on a things-shown-to-the-children style of presentation.

But although the success story of child art was widely acclaimed for a long time it was not obvious how, if at all, the new approach could be applied to the teaching of the regular examinable school subjects, least of all those like mathematics which exhibited a built-in logical structure and discipline of their own. The self-activity of a seven-year-old messing about with powder paints might simulate that of a Matisse – very often the end-products of child art bore an uncanny resemblance to those of the Fauves – but at first it was not obvious that the same method, or any variant of it, could hope to produce comparable results in other fields.

Nevertheless, it is clear that the bridgehead established in the realm of child art was the forerunner of a much wider reform movement which is now affecting the curriculum as a whole. Implicit in its theory and practice are certain common principles. First among these is the recognition of the need to shift the onus of learning, where possible and as far as possible, from the instructor to the pupil himself. The child who has been encouraged to use his imagination freely and to develop his powers of independent thinking will, it is held, bring these qualities to any work he does. What he learns through such activities as painting, mime, or music-making in the infant's classroom will serve him equally well later on whether or not his maturer interests lie on the side of the sciences rather than the arts because they form part of his personal growth.

A second principle, no less vital, involves recognition of the need to adhere to a developmental approach, always treating the pupil according to the mental–emotional–moral stage of life through which he is passing. A third underlines the importance of bringing out the structure and order in the subject-matter so that what is learned is seen within a framework which renders it more easily intelligible.

None of these principles is in any way novel. As regards the first and second, it may be thought that they serve no more useful purpose than pretentious theorizing about 'making the inner outer' has done in the past. As for the third, its emphasis on structure and relevance may seem to do no more than resurrect that oldest of educational chestnuts, the problem of transfer of training, without throwing too much light upon it either.

Be this as it may, for nearly half a century after the initial breakthrough in art teaching, most schools found it convenient to ignore these principles and carried on with their conventional methods. The fact that in doing so they were concentrating on a relatively narrow range of cognitive skills – as often as not the art of passing examinations – to the virtual exclusion of other aspects of the nurture of personal growth was, to be sure, frequently deplored, but so massive was the force of habit that few teachers were able, even if at times they felt impelled, to resist, let alone reject it. The fact that the long-term effects were observable in the inanities and bingo-style fecklessness of large sections of adult society was too uncomfortable to be faced. So, too, was the thought that much of the disorderly behaviour among the teenage generation might be due to a pent-up protest against a misspent school life, an explosion of energies that had been denied the outlets they needed and deserved. The song of the beat-group, by turns defiant and nostalgic, gives strident utterance to aspirations that have been too long denied, hinting in however inarticulate a fashion at sins of omission in these young people's upbringing. Can it really be the case that,

> in the schools this energy is frustrated by regulations designed to keep masses of young people in order by making them behave in unison. It is frustrated, too, by tired, overworked teachers who cannot spare the time to nurture the creativity of the individual student because they must struggle amid the impersonal web of administrative detail to instill into their swollen classes the basic requirements of a stereotyped syllabus?[5]

The conclusion to which we are driven is that this is precisely what has been happening, and that unless something is done to correct the situation we are heading for serious trouble. As one sociologist sees it:

Our teaching methods, certainly up to the age of 16, tend to demand one right answer and throughout are marked by examinations which encourage standard answers. It may be that we turn children who are potentially creative into adults whose only wish is to succeed through conformity. Psychologists now believe that some people have an innate mode of thinking such that they tend to give the expected answer or follow the usual line of thought, whilst others have a mode that enables them to diverge easily from the conventional. It is suspected that the emphasis in our schools may teach the 'diverger' to think in a more conformist manner and thereby crush potential creativity.[6]

As one psychologist explains it:

In problem-solving, it appears that extrinsic, ego-involved motivations, as contrasted with intrinsic, task-involved motivation, are detrimental both to the ability of the creator to free himself from the constraints of old ways of thought, and to his capacity to produce original insights. In the light of this, part of the reason that conformity pressures may be expected to be injurious to creative thinking now becomes somewhat clearer. The outer pressure and inner compulsion to conform arouse extrinsic, ego-involved motives in the problem-solver. His main efforts tend to become directed toward the goals of being accepted and regarded by the group, of avoiding rejection and punishment. The solution of the problem becomes of secondary relevance, and his task-involved motivation diminishes. In being concerned with goals extrinsic to the task itself, and particularly as rendered anxious about potential threats in the situation, his cognitive processes become less flexible, his insights less sensitive.[7]

As the evidence from research studies accumulates the suspicion that something is seriously amiss in the educational process cannot fail to swell into overwhelming conviction. Typical of the many investigations reported so far is that of Getzels and Jackson, whose findings, well-publicised as they have been, merit the closest consideration.

From approximately 500 high school pupils whose average IQ was 132 two experimental groups were formed: [1] a *High Creative Group* ($n = 24$) who were in the top 20 per cent on tests of creativity but below the top 20 per cent in standardized intelligence tests,

[2] a *High Intelligence Group* ($n = 28$) who were in the top 20 per cent measured intelligence but below the top 20 per cent in tests of creativity. (Pupils in the top 20 per cent in *both* kinds of test were excluded from the experiment.)

In the tests of creativity pupils were posed a variety of open-ended questions or problems e.g.:

'How many different uses can you think of for – A BRICK, A PAPER CLIP, A TIN CAN, A PENCIL?'

'Compose three different endings (moralistic, humorous, sad,) for each of several fables.'

'List all the ways you can think of to improve a toy dog so that children would have more fun with it.'

'Make up as many problems as you can think of that might grow out of having an extremely permissive high school principal.'

Comparison of the performances of the two groups revealed a number of interesting differences:

1] Despite a difference of 23 points of IQ between them there was no significant difference in scholastic attainment.

2] On the whole, teachers preferred the High Intelligence pupils – the High Creatives tended to be regarded as an awkward squad, unruly, unreliable, less amenable to classroom discipline.

3] In the High Intelligence Group there was general agreement between the qualities they admired in themselves and the ones they thought necessary for success in adult life. In the High Creative Group there was no such agreement: as individuals, they tended to be less secure, less happy, more withdrawn and introverted than the others. On the other hand, the High Creatives displayed a livelier sense of humour than did the High Intelligent children.

4] The High Creative Group exhibited more imagination, fluency and originality in their written English.

Clearly, there is no excuse for jumping to large conclusions on the basis of evidence drawn from a small-scale investigation of this kind. Certainly there is nothing here to suggest that children of average or below-average intelligence will nonetheless turn out to be highly creative. All that has been demonstrated is that the possession of a high IQ does not guarantee high creativity. (Subsequent studies, in fact, indicate that the cut-off point above which high creativity can safely be expected is probably somewhere around the 120 IQ mark.)* Educational research workers, moreover, may query the validity of the statistical data on the grounds that the scoring of the tests is as open-ended as the tests themselves, to say nothing of the host of variables involved, which makes any interpretation of the 'results' next to impossible. Measuring creativity with such blunt instruments, they object, is like trying to stick jellies on to a wall.

Even so, the differences between the two groups are so obviously significant that they cannot be accounted for as stemming from faults in the experimental design or from the inadequacies of the available measuring techniques. Neither can they be explained away by saying that the High Creative Group was composed of over-achievers. Like the famous Michelson–Morley experiment, the outcome of which perplexed physicists until the theory of relativity came to be formulated, the Getzels and Jackson investigation awaits its educational Einstein for full and final elucidation.

* 'We may also say that no one can be very low in intelligence score and also very creative. That is the way the scatterplots look. But it should be pointed out that the intelligence-test scores used in these studies are weighted heavily with verbal or semantic content and, for the most part, the divergent-production tests have also been semantic. What of the possibility of being highly creative in *non-verbal* ways in spite of low verbal-intelligence scores? On this question we can speculate.

'Generally, the correlations between figural tests and symbolic tests on the one hand and semantic tests on the other are very low. From this general principle we should infer that the correlations between verbal-intelligence scores and divergent-production scores in figural or symbolic tests should also be low.'

J. P. Guilford, 'Basic Problems in Teaching for Creativity' (unpublished paper presented at the Conference on Creativity and Teaching Media, La Jolla, California, Sept. 1964).

At first sight, it is tempting to conclude that the differences between 'high intelligent' and 'high creative' types is temperamental, equatable with the difference between 'convergent' and 'divergent' modes of thought. If only it were as simple as that!

Leaving aside for the moment the question of how valid a convergent–divergent typology may or may not be, there is cause for concern in the thought that the overall effect of mass education is apparently to produce conformity at the expense of 'growth beyond the type'. It is no accident that the creative pupil is looked upon with disfavour. Never let it be forgotten, either, that the creative teacher also is penalized. In an inquiry carried out in Utah, a group of specialist science teachers were tested for ingenuity and their scores correlated with ratings of their teaching ability obtained from the principals of the schools in which they worked. The correlation was -0.38![8]

The reasons for this stubborn resistance to innovation on the part of educational and social institutions generally are clear enough and need not detain us. Their organization depends on the maintenance of steady states, on the observance of the 'done thing': they abhor deviant behaviour in any shape or form as a disruptive influence which may lead to a big bang unless it is corrected in time. More often than not, what is called discipline in school means the preservation of an apple-pie order in which everyone follows an agreed set of rituals and no one steps out of line. The very names of the cellular units which make up the school's structure – 'grades', 'classes', 'standards', 'forms' – bear witness to its addiction to common-denominator methods of handling the young. Since promotion is by seniority, too, it is only to be expected that in the ordinary way of things most headmasters should play safe, not that there is any point in pretending that they function as a gerontocracy – old dogs who are incapable of learning new tricks – but because the nature of their responsibilities necessitates the preservation of an established order.

For his part, too, the administrator is inclined to look askance at the would-be innovator. The odd-man-out irks him. As the author of *The Organization Man* points out, 'The creative individual he does not understand, nor does he understand the conditions of creativity. The messiness of intuition, the aimless thoughts, the impractical questions – all these things that are so often the companions to discovery are anathema to the world of the administrator. Order, objective goals, agreement – these are his desiderata.'

Granted, there are plenty of honourable exceptions to the rule – go-ahead directors of education, enlightened HMIs and lively headmasters are never in such short supply as to inhibit all possibility of change – but in the main the rule holds; and the rule is that in our kind of school society the cards are stacked against the potentially creative child from the start.

The trouble is that whereas the eminent artist or scientist can be recognized by the work he has done or is doing it is nothing like so easy to identify children who are potentially creative. It is perhaps a sign of the times that most of the subjects selected for case-study so far should have been scientists, but in the absence of any surer aids to identification the character-profiles drawn from such studies are better than none.

> They are persons of high intelligence, of marked independence of judgement, disciplined, introspective and sensitive, with intense commitment to their work. They are very likely to be so preoccupied with their own thoughts that they may seem quite withdrawn. When they were growing up most of them read intensively and extensively, and many pursued long-term planned projects of various sorts on their own initiative. They may have had one or two close and like-minded friends, and the chances are very good that when they were adolescents they were not social leaders nor even much involved in peer-group activities. In school the chances are that they made consistently high grades, but they may have been very erratic in this respect, doing extraordinary work in subjects which interested them and wilfully neglecting others. They may have been the delight of their teachers throughout the school, or they may have been a trial to almost everyone. Clearly they don't match the stereotype of the 'clean-cut American boy'.[9]

This characterization seems to agree fairly closely with the requirements for success in personnel management as indicated in another study. According to this, five factors are involved:

1] Intellectual competence

2] Inquiring habits of mind

3] Cognitive flexibility – i.e. the ability to deal with new and unexpected situations

4] Aesthetic sensitivity – a deep-seated preference for elegant solutions

5] Sense of destiny – the personal conviction of the essential worthwhileness of the work in hand and of its outcome.[10]

As descriptions go, these are probably as accurate as any we can expect at the moment, though they add little or nothing to the knowledge already gleaned, say, from the literature of criticism or autobiography. The latter's account of how the creative imagination works may well be preferred as being the more perceptive and sympathetic.

Says one philosopher,

> It is the necessity of 'letting oneself go' imaginatively in the early stages of any inquiry, the positive need of a certain amount of reckless daring in breaking away from one's established habits and getting out of the ruts worn by one's past experiences. It is the willingness to take risks, to make leaps in the dark, to try unlikely and apparently absurd mental combinations, and even to be accused of madness by the stodgy, in company with most of the pioneers of thought. When one of the professors at the California Institute of Technology asked Albert Einstein how he came to formulate his famous theory, he is said to have replied, 'By refusing to accept an axiom'.[11]

All of which is very true, only so far as educational theory is concerned we have heard it before – in *Emile*, in *Culture and Anarchy*, in Whitehead's *The Aims of Education* and many other contexts. In any case, honesty compels the admission that even if we were able to identify pupils with creative potential infallibly we do not know enough to ensure that we will be able to help them to actualize it. The one thing we can be sure of is that the possession of high measured intelligence does not in itself guarantee creative behaviour, which evidently requires quite different attributes of mind. It is the acknowledgement of the existence of this unexplained something plus which explains why creativity has come to figure as a kind of Unknown God in contemporary educational theory. The riddle remains, but the hunch – as things are it would be misleading to call it more than that – is that when the riddle's meaning is disclosed it will amount to a revelation.

In the meantime there is solid ground for reassurance, indeed for cautious optimism in the findings of the psychologists and the sociologists. Although the authorities are by no means all of one mind, there is general agreement that the concept of measured intelligence as it has been understood hitherto is too limited and needs to be replaced by a more sophisticated one. The few factors normally allowed for in an IQ test are not the only ones which need to be reckoned with in the educational process, still less in life as it is lived. More often than not, the dominant factor has been one involving verbal reasoning. Seeing that from the outset the school's stock in trade has been largely concerned with literacy it is, of course, only natural that verbal reasoning should have come to be regarded as a *sine qua non*. Most parents and teachers, however, have always been secretly dissatisfied with this simple yardstick of human abilities. This vague disquiet, often amounting to a guilt-complex, now finds articulate expression in the rank and file of psychologists, most vehemently among those who are exploring the field of creativity.

Typical of the *nouvelle vague* outlook is the following admission: 'For a long time I have been troubled about the readiness with which some persons conclude that everything that is not measured by our current intelligence tests is therefore non-intellectual in nature. Too many new and potentially important intellectual factors have now emerged for this type of reasoning to be tolerated any longer.'[12]

In short, the cult of the IQ has had its day and must give way to a more adequate (and hence more complex) model of the structure of human abilities. This is not to say that the IQ measurement is

totally discredited – it has served a variety of useful purposes and
will almost certainly continue to so do in the foreseeable future – but
it can no longer claim to be regarded as a safe arbiter. So long as
it is, we must resign ourselves to the strong probability that our
selection procedures will miss at least two out of three of those
children who are best fitted to become our future leaders.[13] The
fact that most standardized intelligence tests take little or no
account of such attributes as industry, ingenuity, spatial ability,
sensitivity, inventiveness, or original thinking has always been
known (and to some extent allowed for, it is only fair to add, in
most selection procedures). Only during the past decade, however,
has this fact been brought to the forefront of attention where it
can no longer be ignored.

   To begin with, it seemed that the secret of creativity was to be
found in divergent thinking, i.e. the tendency to pursue
unexpected, novel, tangential directions. In convergent thinking,
by contrast, the tendency is to follow a given lead, to obey instructions, to expect only one right answer. For a time it looked as
though there might even be two distinct personality types, akin
to the Jungian introvert and extrovert – and that both of them might
be determined at birth. According to this latest version of the
Myth of the Metals 'divergents' were the creative types, the blue-
eyed boys who were presumably destined to become the leading
artists and scientists, while 'convergents' were the non-creative
types, the dull dogs who were presumably fated to assume the role
of journeymen in adult society. With this as the prevailing view,
it was understandable that Dr Liam Hudson's investigations among
sixth-formers, which showed that those opting for science were
preponderantly 'convergent' while those entering arts courses
were, on the whole, classifiable as 'divergent', aroused considerable
anxiety at the time.

   But in this field, where all findings must be treated as tentative,
second thoughts prompt a less alarmist interpretation. Hudson's
subsequent studies of clever schoolboys indicate fairly conclusively
that the notion that 'divergers' are potentially creative, 'convergers'
not, is fallacious. It seems a pity, indeed, that he should have seen

fit to retain the names, for to do this only helps to perpetuate a non-existent dichotomy. The evidence from the tests shows that in some individuals at least an original turn of mind may be accompanied by a high degree of convergence. For example,

> Hancock, at the age of 16, has built a computer which plays the Chinese stick game 'Nim' against all human comers. He is at the moment building a computer which will teach a ball to escape from a maze – or, rather, it teaches the maze how to allow the ball to escape from it. He is a boy of remarkable inventiveness, with great stamina and a good theoretical grasp of what he is doing. Yet his responses to Uses of Objects are few and banal. . . . The inventiveness of these boys has escaped us more or less completely. And they are not exceptions. Of the twenty-eight boys tested, six could be classified as showing imagination and originality in their technical work; and six others as much more stolid, working with great patience and precision, but without inventive flair. *The differences in test score between these two groups were slight.*[14]

The moral of which seems to be that so long as the diagnostic and measuring techniques available to him are as crude as they are, the researcher does well to beware of labels. In a general way it appears that the twin modes of thinking styled 'convergent' and 'divergent' correspond with those normally referred to as analytic and intuitive. Analytic thinking, at any rate, proceeds explicitly, step by step; intuitive thinking, by contrast, skips about, makes leaps in the dark and has a way of being unpredictable. To suppose that any individual engages in one to the total exclusion of the other is a manifest absurdity. What we have to reckon with is not a straight choice between alternatives but a blend of elements which *together* constitute the individual's peculiar intellectual life. It may be that just as each of us is supposed to be born a little Liberal or else a little Conservative there is usually a bias one way or other; but it is anybody's guess as to what is the proportion between the two 'types' in any population – and anybody's guess as to whether the differences between them are hereditary or due to environmental influences.

Guilford, who has wrestled with the complexities as manfully as any psychologist – and longer than most – at first believed that a combination of seven distinct abilities was needed in order to produce the creative personality. These defined themselves as:

1] Sensitivity – a heightened awareness of problems, of sense impressions, of personal relations
2] Fluency – the ability to produce a flow of new ideas and associations, and to express them verbally or pictorially
3] Flexibility – spontaneous adaptability to unusual, unexpected situations
4] Divergence – refusal to conform, reluctance to comply with the obvious or the given solution
5] Re-definition – transformation of the known into something else not previously known
6] Analysis – attention to significant detail
7] Synthesis – finding meaningful connexions between discrete ideas, facts, or objects (e.g. as in collage).

It will be seen that the list corresponds fairly closely with the two others outlined previously.

Now it is true that some of the more strikingly creative abilities can be classified under the category of divergence. But not all. As Guilford points out,

> One of the creative-thinking abilities mentioned – re-definition – is classified with the convergent-thinking factors, a classification that may seem to be somewhat contradictory. But it is in the row for which the product is transformations. Much creative effort is in the form of transformation of something known into something else not previously known. . . . A sample item: 'From which object could you most likely make a needle?', has the alternative answers, 'cabbage; spice; steak; paper box; fish'. The essential step in solving this item is changing the meaning of an object, or part of an object, in order to adapt it to some new use.[15]

The example chosen may not be as convincing as one would wish, but it makes its point. The creative process does not occur in a vacuum: it must first of all have materials to hand and the mastery of skills to bring it to life. Great Master and great mathematician alike must 'know their stuff', must submit themselves to the disciplines of their trade, before they dare aspire to take off on the lonely adventure of finding paths where none as yet exist. Every Raphael must have his Perugino. Strictly speaking, after all, it is arguable that human beings are incapable of creation at least in the sense that it is impossible for them to make something out of nothing at all: the best they can do is to find new ways of combining existing elements – and to this end they must prepare themselves through the normal learning process. In other words, like everyone else, they must engage in the kind of mental operations characterized as 'convergent'. What distinguishes the great artist and the top-flight scientist from the ordinary run of mortals is the fact that they do not do this most, or all, of the time! The point is that it is a foolish misapprehension to suppose that the act of creation is a bow drawn at random. Divergence that is not nursed and incubated in convergent habits of mind is apt to be sheer lunacy. We remember the brilliant flashes of insight, the Eureka moments: we forget the patient build-up, the long years of waiting in the dark, the dedicated life immersed in its trials and uncertainties, the baffled periods when nothing goes right and the outcome is dubious. True, an Einstein may 'refuse to accept an axiom' and a Picasso may feel free to 'fling a pot of paint at the public', but neither would have made any impact on society unless they had first become past-masters in their chosen profession. But for this, their inability to accept the obvious would have been mere bravado. Any ignoramus, after all, can break the rules; it takes a genius to re-make them. An infinite capacity for taking pains may not always be its obvious hallmark, but it seems certain that what is called the creative act represents the consummation – parturition might be a better word – of a process of development which extends over a longish period of time. Its gestation, apparently, varies from discipline to discipline. No one knows, for example, why it is that most important discoveries in mathematics and the natural sciences have been made

B

before the age of thirty, whereas in the pictorial arts it is not uncommon to find the output of masterpieces continuing beyond
the age of ninety. One can only guess, *a priori*, that the difference
is in the medium, not in the man. Whether or not the two
cultures hypothesis is valid, whether or not the names 'art' and
'science' stand for an actual epistemological distinction between
Geisteswissenschaften and *Naturwissenschaften*, most people would
agree that the *feel* of learning to appreciate poetry is not the same
as that of learning differential calculus. To describe literature as
an intrinsically messy subject may be unfair, but not unfair to say
that it cannot readily be reduced to postulates, principles and
axioms in the way that mathematics can. The one lends itself to
intuitive methods of learning and teaching, the other to a more
analytical frame of reference. Either way, however, both 'convergent' and 'divergent' modes must be thought of as complementary.

Culture, thought Arnold, is the pursuit of total perfection.
Education, thought Whitehead, requires the habitual vision of
greatness. Creativity, by the same token, may be thought of as
self-fulfilment through aiming at excellence. Poet or craftsman,
scientist or shopkeeper, each excels at his own level. Each has his
arete.

Having already cast a disparaging glance at the James Joyce–
electrician comparison it may seem that the argument is about to
contradict itself. But it is one thing to be scornful of the kind of
egalitarianism which would have us believe that the *levels* and
modes of creative activity of the genius and the honest journeyman
are the *same*: it is quite another to believe that these levels can be
raised and these modes of creative activity made more accessible
to the masses. The objection that at present educational theory has
no way of translating this belief into common practice is neither
here nor there – merely another way of saying that educational
theory is itself left facing an open-ended situation. It is not simply
that as standards of achievement rise the ceiling of educability is
being raised. The lid has been removed once and for all. Twenty
years ago it was thought wildly impractical to say the least, to try

to teach set theory or a foreign language in the primary school. Twenty years hence who dare say what startling revisions of our received opinions will be forced upon us?

Before optimistic conjecture gets the better of sound judgement, however, it is necessary to remind ourselves that there is nothing in the evidence so far to warrant the hope that the average child

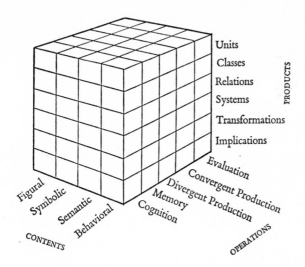

FIG 5 Theoretical model for the complete 'Structure of Intellect'. Department of Psychology, Project on Aptitudes of High-level Personnel, University of Southern California, October 1961

will ever become highly creative. It looks as though any idea that the learner who is not 'good at school subjects' will somehow or other compensate for it by being 'good with his hands' is fated to remain a pathetic fallacy. But even here we must admit to uncertainty. It may be that as we move further and further away from Spearman's 'g' notion of intelligence the optimism now dismissed as wishful thinking will be justified in the event.

Certainly this is the direction in which our thought is moving. The three-dimensional theoretic model of the structure of intellect proposed by Guilford and his associates may not meet with universal approval but at least it represents an advance on the crude models to which we have been accustomed. It is superior [1] because it attempts to embrace the whole gamut of intellectual activities, not simply the sector of 'pure' intelligence; [2] because it recognizes that in many, if not all, of these activities we are back to learning problems, i.e. intellectual abilities are largely acquired.

Of the 120 different abilities which the 'structure of intellect' hypothesis envisages, Guilford claims to have isolated more than 70 by factor analysis. These abilities are classified under three headings: [1] Operations, [2] Contents, [3] Products.[16]

Operations comprise five fundamental types of mental activity:

1] Cognition – discovery, re-discovery, recognition
2] Memory – retention of what has been cognized
3] Divergence – thinking in varied, unconventional directions
4] Convergence – following information that leads to one right answer
5] Evaluation – judging the correctness or adequacy of what we know.

Contents involve the material ('mind stuff'?) in which the activity is engaged:

1] Figural – sense of form, colour, texture, etc
2] Symbolic – concepts of number, etc
3] Semantic – verbal meanings or ideas
4] Behavioural – not clearly defined but broadly equivalent to social intelligence.

PRODUCTS

When a certain kind of operation is applied to a certain kind of content, as many as six general kinds of products may be involved. There is enough evidence to suggest that regardless of which combination of operation and content is concerned the same six kinds of products may be found associated. . . . So far as we have determined by factor analysis, these are the only kinds of products we can know. Or, stated otherwise, we should be able to identify any item of information as belonging in one of these categories.[17]

The six products are:

1] Units
2] Classes
3] Relations
4] Systems
5] Transformations
6] Implications.

Guilford's rationale, to say nothing of his terminology, is not always easy to follow, least of all when it is summarized so starkly as this. Some of the tests used seem trivial, and the statistical inferences drawn from them less than convincing. Some of the categories – 'behavioural content', for instance – seem so amorphous that it is difficult to accept them as they stand. Nevertheless, the structure of intellect model he outlines earns credit for the rigour of its analysis and for opening up new psychometric permutations. In this field, where even the most enlightened researcher is left darkling most of the time, it hints at a kind of multi-dimensional geometry which looks far beyond the flat-earth postulates of the IQ era. While it leaves much to be desired, and more to be explained, the model helps to throw into relief the combinations of ability which lead one person to become, say, a novelist, another a bridge builder, and so on.

From now on we can expect to see a steady flow of books purporting to deal with the problem of how to teach for creativity. Judging by some of those which have already appeared, the advice proffered is at best general and at worst humdrum; and in places the topic is treated almost as if 'Creativity' were a new subject in the time-table. Torrance offers twenty tips for teachers, among them:

Make children more sensitive to environmental stimuli
Dispel the sense of awe of masterpieces

Provide for active and quiet periods
Make available resources for working out ideas
Develop a creative classroom atmosphere
Develop adventurous-minded teachers[18]

– to each and all of which the obvious comment is, 'Easier said than done'.

The thought persists that in the final analysis no one yet knows how best to educate for creativity. It is like asking, 'Can virtue be taught?'

While professing a Socratic ignorance, however, we are by no means clueless.

1] We know a good deal about the characteristics of the highly creative pupil. We also know that if and when he comes to our notice the chances are that he will appear as a misfit.

2] We know that the conditions of school life are on the whole unfavourable to creativity, and that this is because the organization, curricula, and methods stress impression rather than expression – the ability to reproduce rather than to produce. We know also that there is widespread dissatisfaction on this last score. The charge of peddling inert ideas is only too familiar. So is the criticism that school-leavers and university students are competent enough in carrying out routine tasks which involve the application of the techniques they have acquired, but often strangely inept when called upon to tackle problems which call for original conceptualization and generalization.

3] We know that the world of the near future will demand people with greater adaptability than is needed today, adaptability not only in the vocational sense but also in the sense of knowing how to make effective use of their leisure.

4] We must assume, even if we cannot be said to know, that the creative urge exists in some measure in all children. We can be sure, moreover, that this latent urge has hitherto been neglected in the regimen of most schools.

5] The indications are that education can do a great deal to promote the nurture of personal growth by preparing children to become in one way or other creative. As to whether or not education can do anything to increase the individual's natural aptitude in this respect we need to preserve an open mind. The new concept of educability affirms that it can.

6] Education can foster creativity in three main ways: organizational, curricular, and methodological.

A. ORGANIZATIONAL

The internal organization of the school can be changed. Its formal egg-box arrangement of classrooms and time-tabling can be made more flexible so as to allow more opportunities for engaging in individual interests, more private tutoring, more participation in small group activities, more freedom for pupils to 'shop around' and try their hands at leisure-time pursuits which might otherwise never occur to them, more intra- and extra-school societies, etc. Team-teaching represents one example of this approach.

B. CURRICULA

In the overall strategy of any major curriculum revision there are four requirements which normally make themselves felt in the following order:

1] Defining the objectives of the course
2] Determining its content
3] Writing textbooks, providing equipment and supplementary aids to teaching the new subject-matter
4] Re-training teachers in the use of the new subject-matter and new materials.

Of these, the task of writing first-class textbooks is as important as any. The Nuffield Science Project represents one example of the kind of concerted attack on the problem that is needed. In the USA, where the efforts of the School Mathematics Study Group have stimulated similar projects in several other subjects, and on a truly massive scale, both the output and the improvement of textbooks proceed apace. The energy and determination displayed in this concerted drive, with university scholars and school teachers joining forces, springs from the conviction that no matter how difficult the subject is there *is* a way of making it meaningful even to the meanest intelligence.

As one of the prime movers in the 'New' Mathematics explains,

> The word 'understand' and its close relative 'meaningful' have been bandied about in educational circles to the point where just about everyone pledges allegiance to the goal of teaching meaningful and understandable mathematics. We have tried to translate these words into operational terms. We believe that a student will come to understand mathematics when his textbook and teacher use unambiguous language and when he is enabled to discover generalizations by himself. These two desiderata – discovery and precision of language – are closely connected, for new discoveries are easier to make once previous discoveries are crystallized in precise descriptions (it is easier to solve equations when you know what an equation and a variable are!), and skill in the precise use of language enables a student to give clear expression to his discoveries.[19]

Lucid exposition, then, is not the sole hallmark of the new-style textbook. No less vital is its use of if . . . then reasoning which ensures that at all stages the learner is given practice in logical inference – 'thinking for himself'.

C. METHODOLOGY

Here again, the accent is on discovery. The need for carefully ordered, stimulating presentation is in no way minimized, but the insistent requirement is that it must not take the form of a closed system. All courses need to be planned as adventure courses!

To say that all this is not going to be easy is a prize understatement. For one thing, it is going to cost considerable sums of

Number work, with Cuisenaire rods, for six- and seven-year-olds

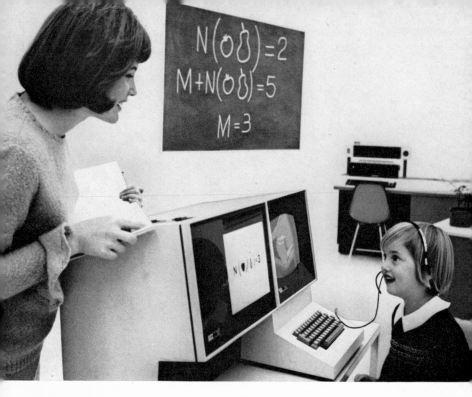

Experiment in computer-assisted instruction (IBM 1500): the new mathematics at primary level. The computer presents statements and questions by means of a viewing-screen, image-projector and audio system. The student types her answers or uses a light-pen to identify information on the screen. The system meets an incorrect answer by providing a fresh sequence of instruction until the subject-matter is mastered. (Photo: courtesy of IBM.)

Nuffield Physics Project. A first-year experiment to find the size of a molecule of oil by measuring the size of a film one molecule thick, formed from a single drop of known volume.

Team-teaching: the nature of sound. Music and science teachers explain the working of the vocal chords by an experiment with rubber bands.

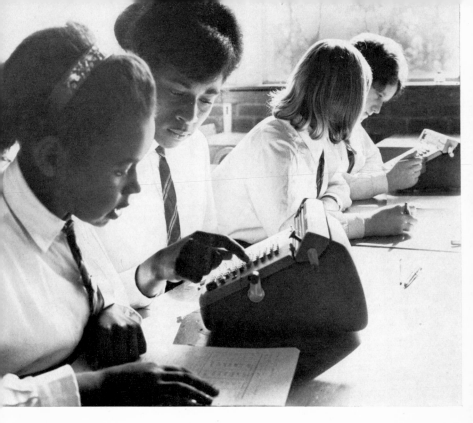

Mechanization in the secondary school: desk calculators and an Autotutor

money. For another, its implementation presupposes a wholesale change in our existing value systems – another way of saying that it is extremely doubtful whether public and professional opinion is at present sufficiently convinced of its worthwhileness.

But enough of speculation. What would an actual 'high creative' school look like, and just how would it function, it may be asked? For once, fortunately, there is an exemplar ready to hand. An absorbing account of it will be found in *Experiments in Education at Sevenoaks*, a book which eschews 'the theorizing that is an occupational hazard for all educationists' (*touché*), preferring instead what it calls 'a stony particularization'.[20] The changes described are part of a quiet revolution in methods, techniques, organization, and attitudes which is, of course, taking place elsewhere and on a wide front. The six sets of activities discussed by members of the Sevenoaks Grammar School staff include Art, the Voluntary Service Unit, the New Mathematics, Creative English, the Technical Activities Centre, and the International Centre.

Each of these is inspired by the same basic philosophy. Thus, the Technical Activities Centre is specially designed so as to provide the same kind of setting for spontaneous, whole-hearted activity as does the playing field. Its facilities cater for the spare-time interests of any boy with an inventive turn of mind. It is the kind of place one can drift in and out of more or less as one pleases. What goes on there is done not for the sake of vocational training, nor as a public schoolboy's concession to the machine age, but because it is conceived of as adding a new facet within a liberal education.

> In every epoch of human evolution there have always been specific growth-points – realms of activity from which the main changes emanated and within which there existed at the time the greatest scope for creative thought, development and adventure. In our time, most though by no means all of these growth-points lie in the realm of science and technology. We can ignore these facts only at our peril. . . . Traditional school science deals with the analytic function of science, i.e. the acquisition of knowledge through the analysis of facts and figures. What is left out of the boy's experience is the

creative use of this knowledge, the creative synthesis. And yet, is not this the more important? Surely all knowledge derives its value ultimately from the creative use to which it is put.[21]

Similarly in the Art room (which is *always* open):

Once inside, the well-ordered convention of the classroom breaks down as the materials and equipment are easily accessible to all, even the smallest boy. . . . The clutter of pieces of iron, piles of assorted collage material and twenty-five boys moving purposefully in different directions, presents a maze that must be navigated before a pattern of working establishes itself to the new boy. As well as the result of working without concern for time and space, this clutter is a starting point: it impels investigation. It is an environment in which he can become involved.[22]

Again, in the Voluntary Service Unit boys are given opportunities of doing odd jobs for old people, helping spastic children and invalids, or acting as traffic wardens. Besides the moral training that comes from introducing them to the idea of a life of commitment, these activities are invaluable in furthering the process of self-discovery. In addition, they serve to alleviate the discontinuity between the school life of the adolescent and that of adult society – 'the yawning gap' between the rising and the older generations.

A great many boys feel that for far too long they are barred from doing anything useful or practical. It is as though having extended dependent babyhood through years undreamt of by previous generations we have devised compulsory secondary education to help with the baby-sitting. Their clubs, their games, and even their studies must seem at times like taking part in an eternal ritual dance only remotely, symbolically related to the hunt they will take part in – one far-distant day. A Voluntary Service Unit can provide the sort of boy who asks those ghastly questions about *purpose* with the actual experience of being useful.[23]

As regards sceptics who ask such ghastly questions as 'What is the point of trying to teach for creativity?', and the most ghastly of all – 'How is it to be done?' – it may be thought that between them the Sevenoaks staff have said it all. In the final analysis, what we are referring to when we speak of creativity is not a method but an attitude of mind. It is an attitude which insists that none of us knows what he is capable of until he tries.

In this freshening spirit, the educational theorist is permitted to pitch his hopes higher than ever before, if not to the extent of affirming that all things are possible then at least that more and more means better and better. For the teacher who is worthy of his hire no other manifesto of faith will suffice nowadays. It is a time for daring.

REFERENCES

1 J. S. Bruner *The Process of Education*, Harvard University Press, 1960
2 Liam Hudson *Contrary Imaginations*, p. 101, Methuen, 1966
  G. F. Kneller *The Art and Science of Creativity*, p. iii, Holt, Rinehart and Winston, 1965
3 G. F. Kneller ibid., p. 11
4 V. Lowenfeld 'Creativity: Education's Stepchild', *A Source Book for Creative Thinking*, p. 14, ed. S. J. Parnes and H. F. Harding, Scribner's, 1962
5 G. F. Kneller op. cit., p. 99
6 P. W. Musgrave *The Sociology of Education*, pp. 138-9, Methuen, 1965
7 R. S. Crutchfield 'Conformity and Creative Thinking', *Contemporary Approaches to Creative Thinking*, p. 125, Atherton Press, 1962
8 Calvin W. Taylor *The Identification of Creative Scientists*, University of Utah Press, 1959
9 Anne Roe *The Creative Student in the Classroom* (Biological Sciences Curriculum Study Bulletin No. 2), p. 2, American Institute of Biological Sciences, 1962
10 Harrison G. Gough *Proceedings of First Conference on Research Developments in Personnel Management*, University of California Institute of Industrial Relations, 1957
11 H. A. Larrabee *Reliable Knowledge*, p. 130, Houghton Mifflin, 1964

12 Calvin W. Taylor 'A Tentative Description of the Creative Individual', *A Source Book for Creative Thinking*, p. 175, Scribner's, 1962

13 Cf. E. Paul Torrance *Guiding Creative Talent*, p. 5, Prentice-Hall, 1962

14 Liam Hudson *Contrary Imaginations*, pp. 48–49, Methuen, 1966

15 J. P. Guilford 'Creativity: Its Measurement and Development', *A Source Book for Creative Thinking*, pp. 162–3, Scribner's, 1962

16 Ibid., pp. 160–61

17 Ibid.

18 E. Paul Torrance *Guiding Creative Talent*, Prentice-Hall, 1962

19 Max Beberman 'An Emerging Program of Secondary School Mathematics', *New Curricula*, p. 11, ed. R. W. Heath, Harper & Row, 1964

20 *Experiments in Education at Sevenoaks*, Introduction, Constable Young Books, 1965

21 Ibid., pp. 61–62

22 Ibid., p. 11

23 Ibid., p. 34

CHAPTER THREE

Team-teaching

===

'Oh boy, is that a loused up mess!' (*Science teacher acting as team leader in a junior high school.*)

'Fine and dandy! If I had to go back to that crummy old classroom – working on my own all the time, I mean – I'd resign tomorrow.' (*Elementary school teacher with thirty-five years' experience.*)

'There's a different spirit in the school since we changed over to team-teaching. It's more demanding for students and more stimulating for teachers.' (*High school principal.*)

'Too confusing. The kids don't know where they are half the time and I guess the staff don't, either.' (*High school principal.*)

'A working model of democracy. The Open Sesame to better schools.' (*District school superintendent.*)

'A bandwaggon for those who think they can get to-morrow's schools today.' (*City superintendent of schools.*)

Representative or otherwise, these random comments serve as a reminder that many American teachers and administrators view the introduction of team-teaching with mixed feelings. This is hardly surprising. For one thing, the organizational changes which are loosely lumped together in the name of team-teaching answer to no set pattern and cannot be reduced to any rule of thumb. For another, the rationale behind these changes is often unclear, and the literature which purports to outline it less than convincing – 'a curious mixture of hortatory confidence and unsupported optimism'. Where team-teaching has been tried out – and the latest (1966) estimate indicates that something like three out of every ten pupils in the USA are affected in one way or other – the vast majority of schools have scarcely got beyond the initial stages of planning. In nearly every case they are still feeling their way towards a new *modus vivendi*, and doing so on a trial and error basis. Even the much-publicized Norwalk Plan, initiated in 1958, has not advanced beyond the proving stage. Not only are the existing plans highly tentative, they are so diverse that it is not obvious how any one of them can be taken as a prototype. Since conditions vary from place to place and from staff to staff, the problems facing each school are *sui generis*, so that no single, common solution is possible.

If there is one common feature it is the insistence on the need for closer co-operation and joint enterprise on the part of the school's staff. To begin with, this creates its own difficulties. 'Commitment to the team philosophy is essential and this involves a certain amount of personal sacrifice. But, then, the advantages as far as the students are concerned are so great', says one school principal. Obviously, however, the changeover from a routine based on a one teacher : one class formula to an organization which calls for the pooling of the school's human and material resources is not always a smooth one. Even in a culture where 'togetherness' is supposedly the ruling passion and 'shared experience' still the only acceptable norm of good conduct there are many teachers who are jealous of their privacy. To give a lesson in front of their colleagues is, for some, an unwelcome experience; they resent having to hand over 'their' class to others; and to have to fall in and fit in with a combined operation (even one which has been formulated and agreed upon in a free discussion), does not always suit their style. It may be true, as the advocates of team-teaching are fond of saying, that individuals who do not take kindly to these innovations are more often than not the inefficient ones: the others quickly adapt themselves to the new situation and find it both more invigorating and more rewarding. Even so, the initial fear of loss of autonomy is not to be minimized.

In any case, it may be remarked that there is nothing about teacher co-operation itself which will guarantee that the last state of education will be any better than the first. As one critic points out,

> The key to effective communication among members of a team is speaking a common language with respect to educational goals and with respect to methods of achieving them. If this common language is to prove adequate for planning and evaluating instruction it must be sufficiently explicit to provide a basis for locating points of agreement and disagreement about educational goals and to enable team members to decide upon specific instructional procedures that are intended to accomplish specific learning outcomes with students. We have every reason to doubt that today's teachers speak this sort of common educational language. They do not agree on the essential purposes of education.[1]

This is not the only caveat which needs to be made, either. It must be stressed that the conditions which have given rise to the team-teaching movement in the USA in recent years are very different from those prevailing in British schools, and that for this reason alone it is extremely unlikely that comparable developments in this country will follow the emergent American pattern. The cross-cultural differences are certain to prove a more serious barrier than they have done, for example, in the case of programmed learning. The trans-Atlantic brand of team-teaching is emphatically not for export.

But to sound a cautionary note is not the same as to conclude that there is nothing to be learned from the infectious enthusiasm of a movement which has spread like wildfire since its inception in 1956. Any reform which seeks to de-bureaucratize the school's way of life deserves serious consideration.

What, then, is team-teaching? Most of the available definitions, unfortunately, are singularly unhelpful. Team-teaching, we are informed, 'is a type of instructional organization, involving teaching personnel and the students assigned to them, in which two or more teachers are given responsibility, working together, for all or a significant part of the instruction of the same group of students'.[2]

British teachers, encountering this bald definition for the first

time may well react as M. Jourdain did on learning that he had
been speaking prose all his life. Surely, this – or something very
like it – is what we have been doing all the time, they will protest.
What else is a harmonious school staff, if not a team, they will ask?

Alternatively, team-teaching is said to be 'an arrangement
whereby two or more teachers, with or without teacher aides,
co-operatively plan, instruct and evaluate one or more class groups
in an appropriate instructional space and given length of time, so
as to take advantage of the special competencies of the team
members'.[3]

This takes us a little closer to the heart of the matter, but still
leaves too much unexplained to be really satisfactory. Indeed, there
seems to be little point in seeking a definition that will be
meaningful. Instead of asking what team-teaching is, it is much
more useful to ask what happens in a teaching team. Thus
rephrased, the answer to the question becomes a good deal clearer.

'A teaching team is a systematic arrangement wherein several
teachers, with a leader and assistants, and with an optimum use of
technology, co-operatively instruct a group of students, varying
the size of the student groups and procedures with the purpose of
instruction, and spending staff time and energy in ways that will
make the best use of their respective competencies.'[4]

This at least has the merit of mentioning some of the guiding
principles in team teaching. These principles may be listed as:

1] *The size and composition of the group must be appropriate to its
purpose*
For some purposes it may be most convenient and most
effective to assemble two or more classes of pupils. For others,
much smaller groupings are desirable. For others again,
individual tutoring and private study are essential. For some
purposes, 'streaming' and 'setting' may offer the best solution.
For others, mixed ability groupings may be preferred. It is
an illusion to suppose that reduction in the size of classes will
act as a panacea. There is no magic number, whether it be
30, 25, or 20, for calculating the 'right' size of the class. The

number may be 200, 20, or 1 according to the needs of the learning situation. The concept of the fixed-size class is obsolete.

2] *The time allotted to any group must be appropriate to its purposes*
A fairly fluid time-table is essential. Since the pupil's interests cannot be switched on and off at the drop of a hat, it follows that all 'lessons' should not be of the same length.

3] *The learning environment must be appropriate to the activities of the group*
For 'straight' lessons the conventional classroom may still be the best place. But it is not the only learning place that is needed. Laboratories, libraries, workshops, listening and viewing rooms, and individual study carrels are also needed. The physical lay-out of the typical school rarely provides adequately for these.

4] *The nature and extent of the supervision of the group's activities depends upon the purpose of the group*
So long as 'chalk and talk' remains the rule, the arrangement whereby one teacher takes charge of the class works tolerably well. But there are many situations where the teacher cannot be expected to carry on single-handed. As occasion demands, he needs the assistance of his colleagues, either as consultants or as actual fellow workers.

5] *The duties assigned to teachers must be appropriate to their special qualifications and interests*
A teacher who is a first-rate lecturer may not necessarily make a good leader of a discussion group or find remedial work with backward pupils his *métier*. Some teachers have a flair for expounding their subject to a large audience, others for sympathetic attention to the individual pupil's difficulties. Ideally, every teacher should assume the role for which he is best fitted.

6] *The level and style of instruction must be appropriate to each learner in the group*
While not denying that some of these principles have been

F

observed in traditional-type schools, the proponents of team-teaching take the view that the time has come to stop paying lip-service to them. If the new concept of educability is to be lived up to, they argue, due attention must be paid to individual differences. It is not good enough to place the pupil under a single teacher along with 30 or 40 (let alone 50!) other children all the time. Whatever the subject, he needs to be exposed to instruction from several angles and from different viewpoints. As well as paying attention to formal 'lessons' he needs to participate in small-group activities and to work on his own. This cannot be done so long as the conventional school organization is retained.

'School bells begin and end the day and punctuate the beginning and ending of each class period. School scheduling as presently practised usually locks library and laboratory for individual students except during brief periods of the school day. Instruction in each subject is cut and tailored until each unit fits a pattern of orderly administration.'[5]

All children need opportunities to form inquiring habits of mind, to find themselves in learning situations in which they are free to go it alone, but far too often such opportunities are denied by a rigid stop-go-stop time-table. They also need opportunities to learn how to participate effectively in discussion and other joint enterprises, but the formal lay-out of the classroom usually makes it difficult to arrange for this satisfactorily, even if it does not forbid it altogether. Above all, children need exercise in the most difficult of all arts – human relations. Despite the progress which has been made in the development of sociometric techniques, the set-up in most schools has been strangely slow in accommodating itself to this fundamental need – or even to acknowledge that it *is* fundamental.

So much for the child-centred side of the argument. As regards the teacher's interests, the argument maintains that team-teaching offers the best hope of securing full professional status and of off-setting the persistent threat of low morale. Teachers who work out

their plans together and put them into effect in the light of circumstances with which they (and only they) are thoroughly familiar
will not only serve the best interest of the pupils, but will also
come to think more highly of themselves. As it is, 'Lack of time
for professional work damages professional pride. About a third
of a teacher's day goes to clerical and sub-professional tasks, another
third to work which could just as well be done by various kinds
of automated devices. A situation that provides only a third of a
day for the performance of work he is trained to do – and finds
satisfaction in doing – contributes little to the morale of a talented
conscientious teacher.'[5]

This is an all-too familiar complaint, to be sure. Staunch
members of the NUT or the EIS will, one imagines, raise their
eyebrows at the remedy for it proposed by some of the leading
advocates of team-teaching. According to this line of reasoning,
only a school organization which allows for the grading of staff
responsibilities can hope to provide incentives on a par with those
offered in the world of industry and commerce. Such an hierarchy
would ensure that top-flight teachers would command salaries
commensurate with their qualifications and experience. It would
enable them as 'master teachers' to supervise the work of assistants,
auxiliaries, student-interns, technicians, and clerical staff. Under
modern conditions, the argument runs, the first step in tackling
the teacher-shortage problem is to face up to the necessity for a
more streamlined division of labour in the schools. The objection
that this means dilution is short-sighted: on the contrary, it is
only by enlisting reinforcements at the sub-professional level that
the educational services can be maintained at full strength – and
the master teacher's status, like the business executive's, assured.

To British ways of thinking, this may seem to be an unexpected,
not to say unsound argument in favour of team-teaching. In the
USA, however, it is often the first to be adduced. In Dr J. B.
Conant's judgement, 'How such schemes will work out over the
years in practice remains to be seen, but team teaching seems to
many the answer to the question of how to attract more of the
ablest college students into elementary school teaching.'[6]

Stripped of its ballyhoo, then, team-teaching may be seen as an attempt to break away from a rigidly compartmented school organization by arranging for a more flexible use of the staff, the equipment, and the premises. It is inspired by a determination to get rid of the 'egg-crate' method of grouping children in classes of uniform size and the tyranny of a fixed time-table. Thus, instead of all or most of the lessons being planned to last for 45 minutes, say, with one teacher in charge of, say, thirty pupils, the school day is blocked out in longer and shorter periods and for bigger and smaller groupings. Several classes may be combined in a kind of general assembly, e.g. for music, to watch a film, to listen to a lecture, or an address by a visiting speaker. By way of follow-up, they may then be split up into small working parties or discussion groups composed of not more than fifteen pupils. As and when necessary, even smaller groups may be organized, e.g. remedial treatment for backward readers or more advanced work for the ablest pupils. Facilities for individual tutoring and for private study may be made available.

The details of these complicated day-to-day arrangements have to be worked out by the teachers concerned, one of whom acts as the leader. Teams may be organized in several ways. [A] At the secondary stage the simplest arrangement is for a number of specialist teachers to join forces in a single subject throughout the school. [B] Another arrangement is for the specialist teachers to join forces but to restrict their efforts to a particular age-group. [C] An inter-disciplinary approach may be attempted, i.e. with subject specialists from different fields working together with a mixed age and ability group. [D] An inter-disciplinary approach, but confined to a narrow span of ability.

Once selected, teams may be organized on a hierarchical or an equal status basis. Usually, but not always, the team leader figures as a 'master teacher', the one who is responsible for most of the 'straight' teaching of the group as a whole while the follow-up work is in the hands of his assistants. One of the advantages of this, it is claimed, is that every pupil has the subject-matter explained to him by more than one teacher. Under the general direction of its leader, each member of the team is supposed to undertake the kind of work for which he is qualified and best suited.

Obviously, it is much easier to adduce reasons for thinking that team-teaching will never work than it is to demonstrate just how it can be done. Questions about who-does-what-and-when are not the only ones which are liable to cause trouble. As every head teacher knows, the smooth running of a school – even if it happens to belong to the 'egg-crate' genus – calls for tact and diplomacy. To plan on the basis of mutual co-operation presupposes a tremendous amount of give and take, and a goodwill which cannot always be taken for granted. In addition, it necessitates the delegation of responsibilities which, in British schools, are normally thought of as being reserved for the head teacher, whose decision is overriding and final.

It seems that one of the gravest weaknesses in the team-teaching movement to date has been its blithe disregard of the dynamics of small groups. The staff of a school does not function in quite the same way as do the members of, say, a football team, still less with the closely-knit liaison of an aircraft crew. The latter's division of labour is so precisely defined that questions about who-does-what-and-when never arise. Strictly speaking, such a team is a technological task force which operates as a human machine. It is identified by certain characteristics:

1] It serves a single, specific purpose
2] It is highly structured
3] It depends on continuous, instantaneous communication between its members
4] It depends on the co-operation of specialists whose duties never overlap
5] It depends on each of its members' carrying out these duties with maximum efficiency
6] It permits of no deviation from standard procedures (since even a momentary aberration may cause total disaster)
7] It can be given specific guidance based on a task analysis of the team's performance.[7]

By comparison, the staff of a school functions more on the lines of an informal working-party. Among other characteristics, the following may be enumerated:

1] It serves a number of complex purposes
2] It has a relatively loose structure
3] The ascription of roles and the duties assigned to its members tend to be assumed rather than designated
4] It depends to a great extent on the independent contributions of individuals, each of whom is expected to use his own initiative
5] It continues to function despite the inefficiency or absence of one or more of its members
6] It cannot be given much specific guidance.

Having said this, it is necessary to remind ourselves of some of the ways in which the teacher's autonomy within the sanctum of the self-contained classroom is being whittled away. There is, first, the relentless pressure for greater specialization. There is also the ever-growing tendency to resort to instrumentation – the mechanization of the classroom. The days of the all-purpose teacher are numbered. As things are, it may seem merely far-fetched to pretend that the school staff situation bears any resemblance to that of an aircraft crew. But if and when the new technologies of instruction become accepted into standard practice the inaptness of such a comparison will gradually disappear.

What happens in the television studio illustrates the kind of development which is taking place less obviously but no less surely in the schools. Even the simplest television programme is not the work of a one-man band: it is the outcome of a co-operative effort involving a producer, a floor manager, at least one camera man, as well as the presenter ('teacher') himself – who is often left feeling that he is the least important person present. True, some of these roles can be duplicated, but there is no getting away from the differentials imposed by the technology of televisual communication; and if the resources of the medium are to be fully exploited we can be sure that this division of labour will become still more precise. Thus, the best script-writer is not necessarily the best person in the eye of the camera. The would-be teacher, like the producer, floor manager and the others, has to submerge his identity in the collective, remaining unseen and anonymous. This is not to say that he loses his identity, nor does it imply that his importance is lessened, for in the studio partnership no single individual is merely a slave to the dictates of others. Each has his part to play, and is selected for it because he can fill it, if not supremely well, at least better than the others. Leadership circulates from one to another, each member in turn acting as *primus inter pares*. Because of this co-ordination, the impact on the viewers is greater than it could possibly have been if the presentation had been single-handed. Just as two or three men on a rope can scale cliffs which none of them would dream of climbing alone, so the cameraderie of the studio opens up possibilities which no teacher can entertain so long as he is left to his own devices.*

As the school installs more and more mechanical aids to learning its architecture, its internal organization, and its ethos are bound to be affected. Each and every device changes the teacher's role, however slightly. During a school broadcast, for example, it is the disembodied voice which claims the pupils' attention while he does well to remain silent. When a language-laboratory is purchased it is not long before he finds himself in need of the services of a technician. If a teaching machine is being used, its effectiveness will largely depend upon the quality of the programme he selects. When a special film is to be shown he probably finds it convenient to merge 'his' class with that of a colleague (the more so if the latter is more proficient at handling the projector than he is!).

* 'The degree to which a society elaborates a technology determines the amount of division of labor in the society. The rationale of a technology is that its tools are not such that each individual can be equipped with a full set of them. With technological advance more things are possible, but social and technical organization is increasingly necessary to bring them off. In effect, then, the sense of potency – the idea of the possible – increases in scope, but the artificer of the possible is now society rather than the individual.'

J. S. Bruner *On Knowing*, p. 160, Harvard University Press, 1963.

To say, as we are fond of doing, that auxiliary aids supplement the teacher's work without actually supplanting it is a mealy-mouthed half-truth. To the extent that each of them contributes a something-plus which the man on the spot cannot otherwise provide, honesty compels the admission that it *does* supplant him, however temporarily.

All of which may not seem relevant to the case in favour of team-teaching, though it certainly points in that direction. Among the predisposing factors which are likely to inaugurate changes in the school's organization, none is more influential than technology. None, that is, except the economic factor. It is no accident that closed-circuit television networks are located in big cities; that the schools which get language-laboratories, data-processing equipment, and (fairly soon now) computer-based teaching machines are the big ones. The cost of electronic switchgear apparatus tends to be prohibitive except where it is used regularly and with large audiences. Maximum utilization of resources, apparently, goes hand in hand with the trend towards larger and larger organizational units.

At the same time, such departures as programmed learning open the way to individual tutoring. New approaches to teaching, including those which can be construed as variants of the old Dalton Plan, projects, activity methods, 'setting', etc, are best understood as an attempt to devise a more organic school community.

In the long run, therefore, the chances are that team-teaching (whether or not it continues to be called that) will play a prominent part in the future for one very good reason – because it provides the experimental framework within which all or most of the current reforms can be incorporated and integrated.

REFERENCES

1 Glenn Heathers 'Educational Aims' in *Team Teaching*, p. 358, ed. J. T. Shaplin and H. F. Olds, Harper & Row, 1964

2 J. T. Shaplin and H. F. Olds *Team Teaching*, p. 15

3 J. Lloyd Trump and Dorsey Baynham *Guide to Better Schools: Focus on Change*, p. 5, Rand McNally, 1963

4 David W. Beggs, ed. *Team Teaching: Bold New Venture*, p. 76, Unified College Press, 1964

5 J. Lloyd Trump and Dorsey Baynham op. cit., p. 8

6 J. B. Conant *The Education of American Teachers*, p. 147, McGraw-Hill, 1963

7 Cf. D. J. Klaus and Robert Glaser *Increasing Team Proficiency through Training*, pp. 2–3, American Institute of Research, 1960

'*It is trite now to remark that we are in the dawn of a new technological revolution, and it has been obvious for many years that we are facing an educational revolution. What both of these involve is a* conceptual *revolution. The* Das Kapital *of this revolution was written by Whitehead and Russell* (1910) *over half-a-century ago.*'

Patrick Meredith

From 'Documents, Programs and Topics – Some Observations on Topic Analysis', *Educational Sciences*, Vol. 1, No. 1, February 1966.

CHAPTER FOUR

The New Mathematics

Readers who left school more than five years ago and who discontinued their study of mathematics thereafter are invited to sample the following items before going on.

1] 'Which of the following properties is (are) applicable to both the set of integers and the set of rational numbers?
   a] Between any two of the set there is a third.
   b] There is a least positive member of the set.
   c] There is a greatest number of the set.
   d] There is an additive inverse for each element in the set.

2] 'How many numbers in the set $\{-5, -3, 0, 3\}$ satisfy both the conditions in $|n-3| \leqslant 6$, and $|n+2| < 5$?

3] 'Which of the following represents the shaded portion in the Venn diagram?

   a] $(X \cap Y) \cup Z$
   b] $X \cup (Y \cap Z)$
   c] $X \cap (Y \cup Z)$
   d] $(X \cap Y) \cap Z$
   e] $(X \cup Y) \cap Z$.

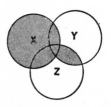

To the extent that they find such conundrums baffling, and the notation in which they are set out incomprehensible, many readers presumably will be forced to admit that recent developments in the teaching of mathematics are nothing if not revolutionary. In no other school subject have the changes in aim, in scope and content, and in methods of presentation been quite so fundamental. These changes, moreover, are world-wide; they arise from the same causes, and despite differences in emphasis from one educational system to another, they are consistent in reflecting a common philosophy.

The foundations of the New Mathematics were laid in the nineteenth century. At the time, the discoveries of such pioneers as Riemann in geometry, George Boole in algebra, Evariste Galois and Georg Cantor in set theory, aroused little interest even in academic circles because they seemed to inhabit a rarefied atmosphere of discourse of their own, detached from all possibility of practical application. Nevertheless, while seeming to lie fallow, they provided the seedbed for the 'Golden Age of Mathematics' as it has been rightly called.

> The work of Lobatchevsky, Riemann and Bolyai, in effect, gave mathematicians *carte blanche* to wander wherever they wanted. Because the non-Euclidean geometries, which were investigated for the sake of what seemed to be an interesting logical nicety, proved to have incomparable importance, it now seems clear that mathematicians should explore the possibilities of *any* question and in *any* set of axioms as long as the investigation is of some interest: application to the physical world, a leading motive for mathematical investigation, might still follow.[1]

Thanks to this release from age-old inhibitions, mathematics has gone from strength to strength in the twentieth century. In the process of becoming more and more abstract, divorced from its possible applications, it has enjoyed a new lease of life. Embracing as it does, many varieties of deductive inference, modern mathematics has invaded fields of inquiry which were formerly thought to be the special preserve of literary intellectuals. On the one hand, for example, symbolic logic has led to important developments in the study of linguistics, while on the other the truth-value calculus has made possible startling advances in computer technology. New branches of probability theory seek to give greater precision to problems which otherwise tend to be so complex as to seem intractable and whose solutions, in the past, have either gone by default or been left to guesswork. Games Theory, Operations Research, Decision Theory, Network Analysis, Communication Theory, and the rest represent attempts to provide mathematical models in terms of which economic policy, industrial processes, military strategy, administrative planning, etc, can be better understood and to some extent controlled. Each offers guidance to decision-making in situations where a high degree of uncertainty is otherwise unavoidable. Mathematics, in other words, has come to be regarded as an indispensable means of reducing the margin of human error to a minimum. From space navigation techniques to the authenticity of the Pauline epistles, the range of problems with which it deals is virtually endless.

Paradoxically, the very remoteness of pure mathematics has turned out to be its chief source of strength.

> Applied mathematicians have been grappling successfully with the world's problem at a time, curiously enough, when pure mathematicians seem almost to have lost touch with the real world. Mathematics has always been abstract, but pure mathematicians are pushing abstraction to new limits. To them, mathematics is an art they pursue for art's sake, and they don't much care whether it will ever have any practical use. Yet the very abstractness of mathematics makes it useful.[2]

Far from playing second fiddle to the claims of literacy, then, as happened during the nineteenth and early twentieth century, 'numeracy' – not quite the word that is needed, perhaps – now figures a good deal more prominently in the school's curriculum at all stages. And here again we are faced with a paradox. Traditionally, mathematics has always tended to be a difficult subject, the kind that few pupils excel and delight in. Being so highly abstract, it might be thought that the New Mathematics would be even more difficult – and in one sense this is certainly the case (as those of us who were brought up under the old regimen soon realize) – yet it appears that children, even at an early age, are attuned to pure mathematical reasoning at levels which were formerly thought beyond their comprehension. Experience has shown that, given the right approach, they can grasp, for example, the concept of infinite sets as readily as most adults. Just as the pure mathematician treats his investigation as a game, enjoyable for the aesthetic satisfaction it affords, so the child's fantasy can be led from free play through rule-bound play to the discovery and eventual understanding of intricate relationships.

Granted, there is no excuse for jumping to the conclusion that from now on mathematics is going to be easy, as accessible to the meanest intelligence as Ludo or Snakes and Ladders. At the same time, readers of such a book as Z. P. Dienes' *An Experimental Study of Mathematics Learning* will be left in no doubt about the viability of some of the new methods of introducing fairly advanced mathematical concepts in the primary school. Quite apart from the novelty of their success in helping young children to tackle problems and solve puzzles which used to be regarded as much too difficult for them, the significance of these methods is best explained in terms of their success in keeping alive the child's sense of delight in mathematical reasoning – delight which was too often killed at birth by the traditional methods.

DISSATISFACTION WITH THE TRADITIONAL COURSES

The growing discontent over the kind of mathematics taught in schools hitherto can be summarized under three main headings: [1] it took no account of the advances made during the past hundred years, [2] it was out of touch with contemporary professional requirements in an industrial society, and [3] it catered for the mechanical application of rules and techniques without fostering any genuine understanding of the mathematical processes involved in problem-solving.

On the face of things, the second of these causes may appear to have been the most influential in bringing about the revolution in mathematics teaching, but all three are interconnected. Even so, if we ask why it is that such topics as matrices, vectors, probability, and statistical inference have found their way into the curriculum of the secondary school, and why set theory is now thought to be an appropriate study at the primary stage, we may as well begin by considering the extent to which pure and applied mathematics have changed the kinds of work we do and, indeed, our whole way of life.

A hundred years ago, the problems facing most professions could be dealt with more or less adequately by anyone possessing a mastery of the four rules of arithmetic. Bookkeeping provides a typical instance. Today, accounting is a vastly more complicated business. The problems encountered in business, industry, and government involve a host of variables and many unknowns, and methods must be devised for solving them on large computing machines. Manufacturing processes, modern transport, and communications have created a wide variety of new jobs – in electronic engineering, radio control, radar, computer technology, etc – which call for the application of advanced mathematical skills.

This is not to say that the traditional mathematics has to be scrapped entirely, or that its only important aspects are the ones which have come to light in recent years. The most telling criticism levelled against the kind of mathematics taught hitherto is not so much that it is antiquated as that it has shown itself to be patently inadequate. Changes in the sociology of knowledge have produced a massive shift of emphasis in every branch of mathematics, as the following passage makes clear.

> Many old subjects are still highly important and we must continue to teach them. Frequently, however, the emphasis must be placed on a different aspect of the subject, and an effort must be made so that the student gains a deeper understanding of it. The teaching of trigonometry and logarithms provides two examples. Trigonometry became a part of the college curriculum in mathematics about 300 years ago when the American colonies were located on the Atlantic seaboard. In the large majority of cases a college graduate became a sea captain, a surveyor, or a minister. A sea captain needed trigonometry for navigation; a surveyor needed it to lay out the farms and

cities of a new continent; and the minister needed trigonometry for astronomy and the calculation of the date of Easter. Trigonometry was the all-important applied mathematics of this earlier period, and the solution of triangles was its important aspect.

Today, the important part of trigonometry is the study of the properties of trigonometric functions rather than the solution of triangles. Radio beams and radar aids have made navigation easy; the new country has been staked out, and only a few, even among the engineers, study surveying; and our observatories now compute the date of Easter. The trigonometric functions, however, have many important applications, for example, in electrical engineering; and trigonometry is still an important subject in applied mathematics if the emphasis is placed on analytic trigonometry rather than on the solution of triangles.

Logarithms were introduced about 300 years ago, and they have been widely taught as an important tool for calculation. But logarithms are no longer important for calculation; small calculations are performed on desk calculators, and large calculations are performed on electronic digital computers. Shall we stop teaching logarithms? Not at all, but the emphasis should shift from logarithms as a tool for calculation to a study of the properties of the logarithm function.[3]

Oddly enough, as the pressure of demand for *applied* mathematics from industrial technology has increased, so has the onus on the schools to find a more effective way of teaching *pure* mathematics. It is the failure to do this which constitutes the gravamen of the charge against the traditional type of course. Time and again, we find the same complaint being registered on both sides of the Atlantic. In England, the School Mathematics Project, initiated by Professor Brian Thwaites of the University of Southampton, has given articulate expression to this veiled discontent. The crux of the matter may be gathered from the views of teachers of mathematics engaged in the Southampton Project.

> In answering a traditional mathematics examination paper a boy has to analyse a problem to discover which of the processes he has learnt are involved. This is a valuable exercise, but it is not exactly mathematics. . . . In making his mathematical application to problems a boy is *using* mathematics, not learning about it. In categorising a

problem and then applying a technique, he is making use of the results of previous generations – who worked out these categories and their associated techniques. No original thought is required at all; there is no discovery. And it is a lack of this, we believe, that makes mathematics for most boys so boring.[4]

An identical viewpoint is exemplified by the policy statement issued by the School Mathematics Study Group in the USA:

A typical lesson might consist of two or three solved examples, followed by a sequence of practice exercises, and students were expected to apply the steps exhibited in the example to get answers to the exercises. The degree of success attained by a student using such tests was a direct function of the student's ability to identify a problem by type and then to apply the appropriate symbol manipulations to obtain the designated answer. The only requisites for successful achievement in high school mathematics were, in many cases, a good memory and a willingness to follow directions.[5]

Traditional methods, it is felt, have erred in being preoccupied with the inculcation of routine skills, in being too content with algorithmic explanations and the manipulation of symbols to the exclusion of any meaningful insight into the nature of mathematical thinking. Being so restricted, much of what was learned was strictly non-transferable. Thus algebra was usually presented as a collection of rules so that its deductive character was less than apparent to the average pupil. Proofs, such as they were, were reserved for geometry, but here again theorems tended to be presented as a set of demonstrations to be followed step by step according to the rules.

In the opinion of one of the most distinguished mathematicians of our time, this is the reason why school mathematics tends to be unpopular and largely unintelligible. The algorithm in arithmetic, the rule in algebra, the theorem in geometry leaves too much unexplained, he thinks. Understanding a theorem does not consist solely of examining each of the syllogisms of which it is composed in succession and being convinced that it is correct. For some people, the convergent types, perhaps, such a procedure suffices.

G

'But not for the majority,' thinks Henri Poincaré. 'Almost all are more exacting: they want to know not only whether all the syllogisms of a demonstration are correct, but also why they are linked in one order rather than in another. As long as they appear to them engendered by caprice and not by *an intelligence constantly conscious of the end to be attained*, they do not think they have understood. No doubt they are not themselves fully aware of what they require and could not formulate their desire, but if they do not obtain satisfaction they feel vaguely that something is wanting. Then what happens? At first they still perceive the evidences that are placed before their eyes, but as they are connected by too attenuated a thread, they pass without leaving a trace in their brains, and are immediately forgotten: illuminated for a moment, they relapse at once into eternal night. As they advance further, they will no longer see even this ephemeral light, because the theorems depend one upon another, and those they require have been forgotten. Thus it is that they become incapable of understanding mathematics.'[6]

If this is not a perfect description of the sins of omission in traditional methods of teaching mathematics it is hard to think of a better. Unquestionably, many people's intellectual life has suffered from an arrested development because, from an early age, they were never allowed to bring 'an intelligence constantly conscious of the end to be attained' to the study of mathematics. For them, as a consequence, it was for the most part a joyless and a pointless exercise. If intuition and imagination are necessary for the advanced mathematician, argues Poincaré, they are much more necessary for the beginner.

> Logic teaches us that on such and such a road we are sure of not meeting an obstacle: it does not tell us which is the road that leads to the desired end. For this it is necessary to see the end from afar, and the faculty which teaches us to see is intuition. Without it, the geometrician would be like a writer well up in grammar but destitute of ideas. Now how is this faculty to develop if, as soon as it shows itself, it is hounded out and proscribed, if we learn to distrust it before we know what good can be got from it?[6]

The New Mathematics is original not only in the sense that it features many topics which were previously not included in the school and college curriculum. As a New Deal, its significance is to be sought in the realm of method rather than that of content. In common with reformers in other countries, the members of the School Mathematics Study Group

> believed that an understanding of the nature of mathematics which, in their view, was not at all discernible in a course in the manipulation of symbols, was needed by every educated person in the twentieth century, and indispensable for any who hoped to engage in work in scientific and technical fields. While they believed that skills were useful, they felt that there was more to mathematics than manipulations. It was their opinion that many of the difficulties encountered by students in their college courses in physics, engineering, chemistry and the like could be traced directly to the overemphasis in high school mathematics on computations and manipulative procedures to the everlasting detriment of the student's ability to use logical inference in any kind of situation whatsoever. The ability to apply mathematics to physical situations seemed to them strongly dependent upon the student's understanding of mathematics itself as the embodiment of logical reasoning.[7]

Circumstances alter cases, of course. In the USA the School Mathematics Study Group represents only one, though by far the largest and most powerful, among a number of concerted efforts to reform the teaching of the subject in its various branches and at different stages. Triggered off by the launching of the first Russian satellite, the main drive for more effective methods and for more up-to-date syllabuses and textbooks has come from the ranks of the academics, that is, from mathematicians themselves – men like Beberman of the University of Illinois, Zacharias of MIT and Begle of Yale – rather than from professors of education. Similar projects under way in Britain and other Western European countries have arisen simultaneously in conditions very different from those prevailing in America. Despite this, they share a common purpose and something akin to a common philosophy; and while they may not always agree among themselves, between them they adumbrate a common theory of instruction.

FRESH APPROACHES TO THE TEACHING OF MATHEMATICS

Any brief account of that theory and its practice will inevitably take an oversimplified form. There are, nevertheless, two outstanding characteristics which set it apart from the theory it seeks to supersede, and which deserve the serious attention of all teachers.

The first is the insistence on the importance of *structure*. If mathematics is to interpret itself as a deductive system, the outlines of the system must be visible from the start and its unifying themes made clear. Such themes include a study of the language and theory of sets, operations and their inverses, number systems and properties of numbers, measurement, graphical representation, statistical inference, probability, logical deductions, and valid generalizations. Some of them are not concerned with numbers at all, yet all involve an understanding of basic principles which is indispensable even at the elementary stage of mathematics learning. In a subject like mathematics, where abstract principles and axiomatic concepts are of the essence, it is vital for the learner to have some frame of reference which will enable him to envisage it as a whole almost from the start. Without this frame of reference he will find it difficult or impossible to see the connexions between the bits and pieces of knowledge he picks up on the way.

In this respect, the New Mathematics may be said to lead the field in the race for curricular reform.

> The curriculum of a subject should be determined by the most fundamental understanding that can be achieved of the underlying principles that give structure to that subject. Teaching specific topics or skills without making clear their context in the broader fundamental structure of a field of knowledge is uneconomical in several deep senses. In the first place, such teaching makes it exceedingly difficult for the student to generalize from what he has learned to what he will encounter later. In the second place, learning that has fallen short of a grasp of general principles has little reward in terms of intellectual excitement. The best way to create interest in a subject

is to render it worth knowing, which means to make the knowledge gained usable in one's thinking beyond the situation in which the learning has occurred. Third, knowledge one has acquired without sufficient structure to tie it together is knowledge that is likely to be forgotten. An unconnected set of facts has a pitiably short half-life in memory.[8]

In general, it is possible to distinguish two approaches to mathematical thinking and learning. The one proceeds from the concrete to the abstract – from things to symbols – and has been called the method of empirical generalization. According to this theory, young children in particular need to undergo a kind of weaning process if they are to be freed from thing-tied thinking; a theory which finds its practical expression in the use of Cuisenaire rods, Multi-based Arithmetic Blocks, geometrical construction kits, and ultimately in the apparatus of the mathematics laboratory.

To the extent that this approach insists that every symbol must have its referent (what it 'stands for'), it can be characterized as semantic. By contrast, the alternative approach is more syntactic. According to this theory, the surest way to make mathematics intelligible is to provide the learner with a basic 'grammar'. To this end, it is argued, the properties of numbers and number systems other than the decimal one should be taught at an early age. The two approaches are, to be sure, complementary. If anything, however, the New Mathematics tends to lay greater emphasis on the second – greater, at any rate, than was thought necessary or expedient in the past.

Another characteristic, and one which immediately strikes newcomers to the New Mathematics, is the importance attached to *discovery*. Instead of being told, 'Do such and such and you will get the correct answer', the pupil is encouraged to educe fundamental principles for himself. If attention to *structure* provides the key to the problem of transfer of training, so attention to the learner's need for discovery, it is urged, will help to fulfil the aim of general education, which is nothing less than training him to think for himself in a disciplined manner. Mathematics is the language of logical inference and must be treated as such from the beginning.

'You gave us an English prep, sir.' The comment of the Sevenoaks boys on being asked to list collective nouns – a swarm of bees, a herd of swans, a pride of lions, etc – typifies the initial bewilderment of many on being introduced to the kind of mathematics which is not concerned with numbers. The idea that an algebraic equation can be read as a sentence strikes them as unfamiliar, while the idea of inequations is even more puzzling. Conditioned to the one and only arithmetic which has been taught hitherto, many learners find it difficult to adjust their mathematical thinking to alternative number systems. Asked to state what is implied in such a statement as '6363 contains 63 twice in one sense and 101 times is another', they are apt to be left tongue-tied. This is not simply because they lack the 'notation' and 'grammar' which would help them to express their thoughts in some sort of articulate fashion, but because the traditional methods for the most part relieved them from the necessity of thinking for themselves.

The New Mathematics is much more meticulous in dealing with fundamental concepts, e.g. the Commutative Principle, so as to make them explicit from the start. But while it insists on the need for a basic grammar and vocabulary, it refrains from laying down the law, preferring, instead, to leave the pupils to draw their own conclusions. Instead of telling him, 'Do this, that and the other and you will get the correct answer', the policy is to ask him, 'If you do such and such what will the logical consequence be?' In this way, it is hoped, the pupil will be encouraged to gain insights into fundamental principles and educe them for himself, somewhat on the lines of Meno's slave boy under the promptings of Socrates.

Which is easier said than done, of course. Meno's slave, it has been remarked, must have been an exceptional pupil – and in any case the Socratic maieutic is not for ordinary mortals. In the wrong hands, undoubtedly, the emphasis on the pupil's self-activity is calculated to lead to some sorry bungling, and until teachers become well versed in the New Mathematics most of them will probably do better to stick to the old tram-lines. Nothing is more certain to produce confusion and mystification in the learner's mind than an abrupt switchover from conventional methods.

In any case, it has to be realized that there is no question of an either-or choice here. Obviously, the pupil cannot be expected to 'discover' mathematics entirely for himself any more than he can be expected to learn to play the piano simply by being presented with the instrument. Bruner makes the point: 'While heuristic procedure often leads to a solution, it offers no guarantee of doing so. An algorithm, on the other hand, is a procedure for solving a problem which, if followed accurately, guarantees that in a finite number of steps you will find a solution if the problem has a solution.'[9] Each has its place. The new approach to the teaching of mathematics tries to strike a balance between the two kinds of procedure – intuitive and step by step – rather than relying exclusively on the latter as was the custom in the past.

The reasons for this shift of emphasis are explained by one of the leaders of the reform movement.

Mathematical thinking, like any other kind of creative thinking, has no predetermined end and cannot be completely mechanised. This does not mean that certain phases cannot be standardised to become quite mechanical. This is what happens when, for example, we use a formula and substitute particular values for variables, or when we transform a formula into another one according to some definite rules of manipulation. It is quite unnecessary to keep in mind all the time exactly what is happening from a mathematical point of view while such substitutions or transformations are taking place, as long as the possibility of interpretation is constantly there, should a non-mechanical step in the form of a decision be required at any stage. The situation would perhaps be likened to the motor skill of walking up a hill; we do not need to be aware exactly of what is happening to our limbs and where our feet are being placed, provided the road is fairly smooth. If the road ceases to be a 'standard' sort of road, the mechanical method ceases to be applicable. If we are climbing up a mountain a rock-climb may be necessary as part of the ascent; and then our awareness of the detailed activity must be considerably higher than during a walk up a 'standard' road. Just as we must be aware of every foothold during our rock-climb, so we should not shrink from employing an even greater degree of mechanisation on standard stretches, such as taking a train, bus, or plane. This is perhaps the best attitude to adopt towards the introduction of teaching machines. There are bound to be people so dazzled by the possibilities opened up by further mechanisation that they will believe that every part of the way is equally susceptible to mechanisation. This should not prevent us from developing a more sober view of mechanisation; it is bound to be appropriate in certain circumstances and not in others (another fruitful field for educational research). The present trend towards programmed text-books and teaching machines merely perpetuates the current rather imperfectly mechanised learning by improving the techniques of such mechanisation. The fault is thought to be in the inefficiency of the mechanisation, and not in the lack of opportunity for the learner to think independently. Although it cannot be denied that subjects can be conditioned into giving certain 'right' responses to quite complex sets of interdependent stimuli, I suggest there is more than this in the learning of mathematics. The exposure to a truly mathematical, open-ended situation is possibly a rather important ingredient of mathematics-learning. If the best way of learning something is by doing it, this surely applies to mathematics; we learn by actually doing, constructing, mathematics, rather than by going through predetermined sequences where each act prompts the next in a mechanically determined way.[10]

While Dr Dienes' main argument is unexceptionable and his criticism of the limitations of Skinnerian programmes almost certainly valid, it seems that he does less than justice to some of the later developments in the field of programmed learning. In fact, the work of researchers such as R. F. Mager, in which the students themselves control the sequence of instruction, underline the importance of keeping the learning situation open-ended. The need for precision in the identification and statement of learning objectives is not the only contribution which the programmers have made to elucidating the problem of 'structure' (incidentally, a problem which lends itself to a solution rather more easily in mathematics than in most other subjects), they are also fully aware of the need for 'discovery'.

Ultimately, the problems of 'structure' and 'discovery' will be seen to be one and the same; and both the proponents of the New Mathematics and the second-generation programmers are converging on such a view. Task analysis, in particular, has thrown new light on the hierarchies and the interrelationships of learning processes which lead to 'discovery', 'insight', 'understanding', and 'total grasp' of a subject. To date, a heuristic method which is at once practical and scientific in the sense that it leaves little or nothing to chance is not available, but the work of devising one proceeds apace. Thus, according to Gagné, learning

> is a matter of transfer of training from component learning sets to a new activity which incorporates these previously acquired capabilities. This new activity so produced is qualitatively different from the tasks which correspond to the 'old' learning sets; that is, it must be described by a different set of operations, rather than simply being more difficult. The characteristics of tasks which make achievement of one class of task the required precursor of achievement in another, and not vice versa, are yet to be discovered. Sufficient examples exist of this phenomenon to convince one of its reality. What remains to be done, presumably, is to begin with extremely simple levels of task, such as discriminations, and investigate transfer of training to tasks of greater and greater degrees of complexity, or perhaps abstractness, thus determining the dimensions which make transfer possible.[11]

MATHEMATICS AND THE SOCIOLOGY OF KNOWLEDGE

While mathematics has figured among the *artes liberales* as a necessary constituent of 'liberal' education since the days of Ancient Greece it is only in recent years that it has come to be looked upon as a *sine qua non*, at least on a par with literacy, in the general education of the masses. This growing ascendancy of mathematics in the modern world is to be understood in terms of changes in the sociology of knowledge, more particularly in the cultural perspective of the last hundred years. To Victorian ways of thinking, certainly, mathematics was for the few: for the many reading, writing, and 'casting accounts' sufficed. In the contemporary situation, evidently, mechanical arithmetic is not enough, even for the beginner: at an early age he needs to be introduced to non-decimal number systems, elementary statistics, probability theory and a host of topics which, more often than not, are beyond the ken of his own parents.

Epistemologically, the overriding importance attached to mathematics in the modern world can be explained as arising from the transfer from rationalistic and empiricistic philosophies to one which is pre-eminently pragmatic. Broadly speaking (but only *very* broadly), these three philosophies may be thought of as corresponding to the prevailing climates of opinion in the eighteenth, nineteenth, and twentieth centuries.

> For the rationalistic tradition, mathematics is the model science. Mathematical truths are general and necessary, and may be established by deductive chains linking them with self-evident basic truths. Demonstration forges the chains, intuition discloses the basic truths. ... Mathematical truths are not dependent on experience though an awareness of them may be suggested by experience. Mathematicians do not need laboratories or experiments; they conduct no surveys and collect no statistics. They work with paper and pencil only and yet they arrive at the firmest of all truths, incapable of being overthrown by experience.[12]

For the empiricist on the other hand, thinks Scheffler, 'natural science is taken as the basic model. Natural phenomena are revealed by experience, they are not disclosed by intuition'. From this viewpoint, mathematics may be conceived of either as 'pure', i.e. representing internal logical relationships among concepts, or as 'applied', i.e. empirical generalizations based upon experience.

For its part, the pragmatic outlook which typifies the modern period stresses the experimental character of the natural sciences and learning from the consequences of such a trial. On this reckoning,

Mathematical knowledge is continuous with logic in the pragmatist's scheme. It is an apparatus useful for elaborating the import of hypothetical ideas, for showing their connections with practical consequences and exhibiting their mutual relationships. It does not itself tell us anything directly about the world, but in bringing order to our array of concepts and in generating their consequences it serves as a regulative instrument of inquiry. Inquiry itself is action, but action regulated by logic and issuing in answers to motivating problems of practice.[13]

Because of this, the ideal education in the second half of the twentieth century is conceived of as one that connects general ideas with specific, actual problems: an education which encourages imaginative theorizing by the student but at the same time seeks to control his theorizing by constantly submitting it to the test of experiment. To this end, mathematics bids fair to become the key discipline, the reigning Queen of the Sciences.

At least educationists who have the future in their bones think so.

The world of today demands more mathematical knowledge on the part of more people than the world of yesterday, and the world of tomorrow will make still greater demands. Our society leans more and more heavily on science and technology. The number of our citizens skilled in mathematics must be greatly increased; an understanding of the role of mathematics in our society is now a prerequisite for intelligent citizenship. Since no one can predict with certainty his future profession, much less foretell which mathematical skills will be required in the future by a given profession, *it is important that mathematics be so taught that students will be able in later life to learn the new mathematical skills which the future will surely demand of many of them.*[14]

IMPLEMENTATION

Obviously, the introduction of new schemes of work needs to be undertaken stage by stage and calls for long-range planning. This is true of any subject in the school curriculum, but especially so in the case of mathematics which demands to be treated as a prestige subject.

In the first instance, this implies not only the recognition of the need for swift and radical changes in the content and methods of teaching mathematics, but also recognition of the need for priority of treatment. Such recognition can only come from the central and local authorities in charge of the educational services. So far as the United Kingdom is concerned, this recognition, if not exactly withheld, has been made less openly than might have been desired. At any rate, the enormous energy displayed in the School Mathematics Study Group and similar projects in the USA (not to mention the enormous funds which have helped to keep them going once they were mounted), has not been matched on anything like the same scale in this country. Here and there, a university or a local education authority has shown mild interest, but for the most part it has been left to groups of individuals, working in isolation, to provide the lead that is needed. The need is nowhere denied, but apparently it is not accompanied by the sense of urgency which prompts immediate action. Nothing short of the imminent threat of war, it seems, can shock us out of our deep-rooted complacency. Educational systems never move so fast as when they are running scared!

Given that the new schemes of work are already drawn up and agreed upon, the administrative problems involved in introducing them into the schools are still very considerable. Among others, they include:

1] The writing, try-out, revision, publication of textbooks and the provision of supplementary aids to teaching
2] The in-service training of teachers
3] The selection of suitable experimental schools and classes
4] Informing parents and the general public about the nature and purpose of the changes
5] Modifying the pre-service training of teachers in colleges of education and university departments of education
6] Providing adequate time and finance during the trial stages (which may last several years)
7] Evaluating the effectiveness of the new schemes of work.

To list evaluation last in the order of priorities may seem an inexcusable breach of faith, but for the sake of getting things done we are left with no alternative. Preliminary findings suggest that the majority of teachers and pupils alike find the New Mathematics more exacting, more stimulating and more rewarding, but beyond saying that it is too early to dogmatize one way or the other. It may be that upon further consideration – as the latest SMSG reports suggest – the highly theoretical nature of some of the new courses will prove too abstruse for the pupil of average or below-average ability. It may be that some of the wordy expressions used to convey basic mathematical concepts – 'Associative Principle', 'Distributive Principle', 'Additive Inverse', and the rest – will turn out to be as empty of meaning for the learner as the symbol-pushing they seek to replace. In the meantime, however, there is nothing for it but to act on the conviction that the general theory is correct and that the practice which flows from it can only be beneficial. For better or for worse, the contemporary world is wedded to a belief in mathematics as a new language, one which enlarges thought and gives expression to it with greater precision and clarity than the world of yesterday deemed possible.

REFERENCES

1 Morris Kline *Mathematics in Western Culture*, p. 431, Oxford University Press, 1953
2 G. A. W. Boehm *The New World of Math*, p. 47, Deal Press, 1959
3 *The Revolution in School Mathematics*, p. 9, National Council of Teachers of Mathematics, Washington DC, 1962
4 *Experiments in Education at Sevenoaks*, Constable Young Books, 1965
5 W. Wooton *SMSG: The Making of a Curriculum*, p. 4, Yale University Press, 1965
6 Henri Poincaré 'Mathematical Definitions and Education', *Science and Method*, pp. 117–42, trans. Francis Maitland, Dover Publications, 1952
7 *SMSG*, op. cit., p. 108

8 J. Bruner *The Process of Education*, p. 31, Vintage Books, 1960
9 Ibid., p. 63
10 Z. P. Dienes *An Experimental Study of Mathematics Learning*, pp. 164–5, Hutchinson, 1964
11 Robert M. Gagné *Psychological Review*, **69**, p. 365, 1962
12 Israel Scheffler *Conditions of Knowledge: An Introduction to Epistemology and Education*, pp. 2–3, Scott, Foresman, 1965
13 Ibid., p. 4
14 SMSG: *The Making of a Curriculum*, p. 108

Just as the 'Three R's' are the essential elements of learning in the early grades, so in the upper grades the three important and interrelated elements of learning revolve around the humanities, the social sciences, and the natural sciences. When we neglect any one, we deprive students of an opportunity for a better understanding of the world in which they live – the world of human beings, the world of the social order, and the world of the physical universe – and we thereby deprive the student also of the opportunity for living a more understanding, a more useful, and a more fruitful life. We used to be afraid to try to teach mathematics and science to youngsters. Now we know these fears were unjustified, for we have found that youngsters have greater capacities than we thought and we have found that the methods of teaching these things are not so difficult as we had supposed. Those who have seen youngsters respond can agree that to them science can be exciting, it can be stimulating, it can be inspiring, and can be of enormous practical value.

Lee A. DuBridge

CHAPTER FIVE

Fresh Approaches
to the Teaching of Science

Can you recall the very first lesson you received in chemistry? If so, how did it compare with this for a start —?

> You are given a sealed black box containing an unidentified object which cannot be handled or seen. You are invited to find out as many properties of the object as you can. As in any other puzzle game, it is left to you to find the solution, only in this case there *is* no solution – the box cannot be opened and one of the rules is that the actual identity of the object will never be disclosed. You can tilt the box from side to side, listen to the noises it makes, estimate the weight of the box itself, and make any guesses you like as to the size, shape, texture and weight of the thing inside it. In doing so, you are, in fact, dealing with an unknown, making assumptions, drawing inferences, using mental models, framing and testing hypotheses, weighing evidence: in short, you are placed in the position of a scientist investigating a research problem.
>
> (*First laboratory session*, 'Observations', *Chemical Bond Approach*)

Or this one —?

> You are seated at a round table together with other members of the class. A candle is placed in the centre of the table and lit. You are asked to watch the flame burning as intently as possible and to make as many detailed, independent observations of the phenomenon as you can. After half an hour of hypnotic concentration you will be lucky if you have jotted down more than a dozen – at which point you learn that a professional chemist's total would amount to no fewer than 53, most of them stated in quantitative terms!
>
> (*First laboratory session, CHEM Study*)

Or this —?

> You are given a generous helping of lawn mowings from the school
> playing field. Can you offer any suggestions as to how the green stuff
> might be separated from the grass fibre? Crush it between your
> fingers? Pound it with a hammer? Try mixing the mess with water?
> See if you can make a solution? Before the lesson is half way through
> you find yourself dropping chlorophyll on blotting paper and be-
> coming increasingly intrigued as you watch the colour rings change
> and spread. Almost without knowing it, you have been introduced
> to elementary chromotography.   (*Nuffield Science Project*)

Quantum mutatus ab illo, the oldsters will reflect: chemistry
teaching was never like this in their day.

Pleasing enough as an opening gambit, the sceptics will retort,
but what does it prove? Has not the shrewd science teacher always
known how to appeal to the beginner's sense of wonder?

Certainly he has; but the shrewder he was the greater the chances
of his being dissatisfied with the aims, content, and methods
imposed on him by course requirements which normally he had
to accept willy-nilly and which he could do little to change. The
reasons for this dissatisfaction may be summarized under four main
headings:

1] The exponential growth of scientific knowledge – doubling
   or more than doubling every 10–15 years – has resulted in
   most school science courses becoming more and more
   outdated. In physics, in chemistry, in biology most of the
   ground covered in these courses is out of touch and (which
   is worse) out of tune with contemporary developments
   in the field of investigation. The distance between the
   frontiers-men and the school-men has been getting steadily
   greater, and so has the time-lag between current research
   and the work done in schools.

2] The attempt to keep abreast of these developments has been
   undertaken for the most part by a process of haphazard
   accretion, adding new bits and pieces to the curriculum that
   was already overcrowded. Because of this, school science has

tended to be a morass of isolated facts and simple generalizations, cluttered with detail and lacking both internal consistency and a clear rationale. Reluctance to discard old material has made is impossible to cover the ground adequately in the time available. In physics, for example, what used to be regarded as the essential groundwork – mechanics, heat, light, sound, magnetism, and electricity – bulks so large in the course as to leave all-too-little room for the kind of topics now claiming attention. All this puts a premium on memorization so far as the pupil is concerned. Principles are lost sight of in the crush, and free inquiry is blighted.

3] Still more telling is the criticism that school science has been presented dogmatically, as a body of facts and truths which had to be accepted, rather than as a method of investigation. Far too many experiments have been nothing better than demonstrations, conducted on lines which led to foregone conclusions. Expressions like, 'We are not sure', 'The evidence is insufficient', 'The explanation eludes us', have been played down and the impression created that the scientists (and the teacher who speaks for them) know all the answers.

4] Most disturbing of all is the idea that school science is intended mainly, if not entirely, for future scientists. Although the battle over the Two Cultures has been fought and won (or lost, according to the point of view), and although it is now agreed that the development of an understanding of the nature of science should be one of the central purposes of education, there is still an aftermath of confusion over the question of how science is to be interpreted as a cultural discipline in its own right. What should be done is not in dispute: how it should be done is less obvious.

Perhaps it was only to be expected that the main drive in the direction of a new outlook and a new methodology should have come, not from teachers (who were in the unhappy position of being unable to do much or anything about it), but from the scientists themselves. Reviewing the causes for disgruntlement which led to the formation of the Biological Sciences Curriculum Study in 1958, Dr Addison Lee writes,

The decade from 1940 to 1950 in science teaching reflected the general education and consumer movements of the 30's and the technical manpower crisis stimulated by World War II. The result was to bring into conflict the function of science in general education and science basic to a career in specialized fields. While the status of science in the secondary school curriculum was never weaker than at the start of this period, the stimulus of the 'Atomic Age' and the acceleration of scientific and technological development following World War II reaffirmed the need for education in the sciences. In brief, the 1940–1950 period represented a decade of divergent points of view about science teaching. Several of the curriculum committees during this period noted the growing enrolment in biology and pointed out that it was the biology teachers who must assume the responsibility of conveying to the majority of youth most of what they will learn about the nature of science.

The decade from 1950 to 1960 has been described as one of 'confusion and crisis' in science education. The relationship between science and technology, especially the part that science plays, is still vague in the minds of most people. The educational controversies of the fifties reflected the scientific revolution, characterised by an 'explosion of knowledge', and the changes in the larger scheme of cultural values in America. The need to improve the laboratory work in biology received much attention. Most of the recommendations were for a more experimental approach to the study of biology. It was during this period that the BSCS studies were initiated.

In many high schools biology consists primarily of either hygiene or animal biology, presented in terms of invertebrate and vertebrate anatomy. Often the emphasis is on memorisation of long lists of scientific names. Biology is generally presented as a crystallized science in which all the answers are known. What passes for lab is often routine cook-book-type exercises or a naming of structures on drawings and answering of questions by looking them up in a text-book. Research biologists who examined high school courses in biology found that: (1) it represented little of the science of biology; (2) it was out of date in terms of today's theories and knowledge; (3) it was fragmented and it lacked logical coherence; (4) it forced memorisation instead of requiring understanding; (5) it did not present biology as a discipline; (6) its laboratory work failed to portray the investigative nature of biology; and (7) it was taught more as a dogma than as an on-going science.[1]

As Dr Lee sees it, the growing demand for a reform in biology teaching stems from a complex of factors and cannot be satisfied by half measures. Since the sheer amount of information existing in each and every sub-field of science is more than can be mastered in a lifetime, nothing less than a drastic re-structuring of school science courses will suffice.

It was to this end that the efforts of the Biological Sciences Curriculum Study, and those of the Physical Science Curriculum Study (PSCS 1956), the Chemical Bond Approach (CBA 1957) and the Chemical Education Materials Study (CHEM Study 1959), were addressed. Inspired by the same sense of urgency which energized their colleagues in mathematics, American professors of science (but *not* professors of education!), industrial scientists, teachers, and administrators joined forces in an all-out attack on the problem. Beginning with a discussion of fundamental aims, they went on to outline new types of course, re-wrote textbooks, laboratory manuals, teachers' guides, and reports for school administrators, designed work-kits, produced films and other aids to go with the textbooks so as to provide an integrated, interlocking set of materials. Apart from their praiseworthy willingness to get together, the most significant thing about these combined operations is the fact that the remedies they propose share a recognizable family likeness. What emerges, as we shall see when it comes to comparing the findings of the various curriculum study groups with the progress reports in programmed learning, is the blueprint for a new pedagogy.

THE BIOLOGICAL SCIENCES CURRICULUM STUDY PROPOSALS

From the start, the Biological Sciences Curriculum Study took its stand on three main points: a secondary school course should

[1] present modern knowledge and concepts, [2] focus on the nature of scientific inquiry, and [3] provide the pupil with a coherent picture of contemporary biology. It would not be simply a revision of old concepts and established ways of thinking. It would place considerably more emphasis on laboratory work, work which would involve genuine investigation on the part of the learner. It would replace styles of presentation which relied on statements of conclusions with those which allowed pupils the opportunity to draw their own conclusions. Where possible, the learning-situation would be left open-ended. Current views on a subject such as genetics would be developed step by step through a description of the experiments performed, analysis of the data obtained, and the interpretations made of them. Less time would be spent on 'straight teaching' and more would be devoted to 'invitations to inquiry', i.e. providing pupils with materials and problems necessitating active participation. Above all, the course would centre round certain basic themes which gave it unity and enabled its underlying structure to be perceived.*

THE PHYSICAL SCIENCE CURRICULUM STUDY PROPOSALS

Here again a threefold requirement was insisted upon. The objectives in secondary school physics were [1] that the course should present the logical interconnexions of the discipline at a level intelligible for high school pupils, [2] that it should treat physics as a product of experiment and theory as created by real people in real laboratories, and [3] that it should show physics as a cultural force of importance to all pupils regardless of their career prospects and ambitions.

> The pedagogical philosophy of the course is to build ideas from very simple observations to more complex concepts, with reinforcement at each point. The films reinforce the textbook, the laboratory work reinforces the films and the textbook. There are many cross linkages among the different parts of the course so that the student's understanding is increased by every available means. One of the major

* Cf. Appendix for details of the BSCS course.

things one notices is that the textbook contains less topical material than the traditional course but provides more penetrating treatment of the material it does cover. The course leaves out virtually all technology; there is no mention of how television works, for example, although this and other technological topics are discussed in the monographs. The course is basically physics for its own sake, the study of fundamental concepts.[2]

THE CHEMICAL BOND APPROACH PROJECT PROPOSALS

Here, too, the similarities in thinking are so obvious that the arguments begin to seem slightly repetitious.

The CBA course attempts to present modern chemistry to beginning students by emphasising the importance of theory and experiment. The presentation is intended to give students a preliminary understanding of what chemistry is, rather than simply an encyclopedic collection of chemical reactions and laboratory techniques. Effort has been made to organize the course in a pattern which reflects the structure of the discipline itself. Since conceptual schemes play a major role in the organization of chemistry, the organization of the CBA course is based strongly on conceptual schemes. An attempt is made throughout the course to confront the student with the implications of logical arguments based on theory. A major part of this is done through the discussion of mental models, which are introduced as logical devices based on a set of convenient assumptions. Particular attention is given to three such models: structure, kinetic theory, and energy. The way in which structural models for atoms, molecules and crystals are developed in the course is illustrative of the approach. First, electrons are assumed to behave as if they were spherical charge-clouds. Under the action of electrostatic forces, these charge-clouds arrange themselves in patterns which can be represented by arrangements of real spheres fastened together. In this way the geometrical relations that govern the packing together of spheres can be used to visualize the arrangement of electrical forces within atoms and molecules. Experience with students indicates that this presentation in the use of geometrical analogies is quite satisfactory.

Such a charge-cloud does not, in its present development deal adequately with energy relations. To improve this aspect, a more conventional electron orbital model is introduced and developed to show energy relationships at least qualitatively. The second model fails, however, in the description of geometrical properties. The orbital model and the charge-cloud are brought together by the introduction of the assumption that orbitals within an atom can hybridize when molecules are formed so as to produce the appropriate geometrical relationships.

Through a discussion of these two structural models, the students get some ideas of the success and limitations of each. One of the aims of the course is to have students realize that it is not proper to ask which are the right models; rather, to judge models on the basis of logical effectiveness for a particular problem. This is presumably the way in which modern scientific discussion proceeds.

The laboratory program of the CBA course is designed to develop the ability of the student to identify a problem, to design an experiment which will shed light on this problem and to carry out the technical operations of the experiment and to arrive at a conclusion through an analysis of his own data. Initially, this student is provided with assistance in all these areas. Such assistance is withdrawn gradually until finally the student is asked to perform all of these steps independently, employing ideas and techniques accumulated in the process of investigating other problems. The sequence of experiments is designed to provide the necessary background.[3]

THE CHEMICAL EDUCATION MATERIALS STUDY PROPOSALS

CHEM Study's original objectives were broadly identical with those of the other curriculum reform groups: to counteract the growing separation between professional scientists and teachers, to stimulate secondary school pupils who intended to go on to advanced study at the university while at the same time furthering the understanding of those who would not continue beyond the school-leaving age, and to devise more effective methods of teaching and courses more closely geared to frontier research. The overriding importance of experimental procedures is signalized in the title of the course textbook, *Chemistry: An Experimental Science*, which is intended to give an overview of the subject, and which is dependent at all points on carefully graded laboratory instruction, supplemented by some twenty-four films shown at specific times during the course.

There is no point in further elaborating the account of these American enterprises, nor of summarizing similar projects in this country which will in any case be well enough known to most readers. Recurrent in them all are a number of common motifs. Even the vocabularies favoured by one are reminiscent of the vocabularies used by the others, and may be thought to provide an interesting exercise in linguistic analysis. The endless harping on 'structure', 'order', 'coherence', 'overview', 'organization', and 'system', for instance, not to mention the preoccupation with 'inquiry' and 'investigation' – and the frequent use of such vogue-words as 'model', 'strategy', 'discipline' or the liking for kindred expressions such as 'logical inference' and 'conceptual framework'. All this, be it noted, not from the pens of educational theorists (the kind of people who are often accused of engaging in speculative fantasy), but from the co-operative deliberations of some of the most outstanding scientists in the business. Accepting their invitation to inquiry, what shall we infer from the evidence presented so far?

First, that the surest way to clear the ground in any scientific field is to do whatever can be done to disclose its underlying *theoria*, and that the indications are that this is true of all fields. If the basic themes, principles, rules, etc, are not known to the teacher in advance there can be no prospect of the course of study for which he is responsible having unity, nor of its revealing the relationships between its parts. Although the curriculum reformers have not gone so far as some of the later exponents of programmed learning have in insisting that it is no less vital for the pupil himself to be clear about objectives from the outset, they have rendered an inestimable service to pedagogy by stressing the importance of outlining the structure of the field of knowledge concerned. While it would be unkind to suggest that traditional school science took the form of things shown to the children, there is some justification for thinking that it was better at talking *about* science than it was at saying what science *is*. Whatever else may be said for or against the new approach to science teaching at least it tries to make up its mind on fundamental issues before it begins.

Amid the flux of theories and the welter of multitudinous items of information the search for constants becomes imperative. The stubborn refusal to admit the finality of scientific 'laws' is accompanied by a strong belief in the efficacy of something which bears an uncanny resemblance to the formal discipline and mental training of yesteryear. According to this, what matters most is not whether the pupil understands the second law of thermodynamics or can reel off the periodic table, but whether he has formed the habit of framing and testing hypotheses, analysing the data he has collected and thinking for himself. The methods of science, in other words, are more than utilitarian: they offer a way of life, the hallmarks of which are intellectual honesty and intellectual penetration.

Allied with this requirement is the conviction that, in all its forms, school science should interpret itself as pure science. This awarding of pride of place to formal discipline is the more surprising in view of the Americans' reputation for being go-getting and gadget-minded, still more so considering the prevailing climate of opinion during the post-Sputnik scare which triggered off most of these curriculum study groups. As happened in the case of mathematics, however, the conclusion reached in every case was that the Russian technocrats had forged ahead not because of any superiority in their training as space engineers but because they had gained more powerful insights into basic scientific principles.

In wishing to see new material introduced into the syllabus, therefore, the new approach to science teaching is not trying to be topical at all costs. Significantly, the PSCS course relegates any explanations of the application of scientific principles to television, radar and that sort of thing to a secondary place in the scheme.

It may be that in trying to put first things first, some of these courses have left themselves open to the criticism that they are more suitable for abler pupils and that they are too high-flown for the average and below-average. As to that, we shall have to see. Tempting as it is to think that most children find it more interesting to dismantle an internal combustion engine or to mend an electric light fuse there is always the danger that this approach to science may not be sufficiently challenging. In pitching its aims as high as it does, the new approach is made in the conviction that a way of making first principles clear to all pupils – 'academic' and 'non-academic', future scientists and non-scientists – can be found if only we try hard enough. Efforts to bring out the structure behind the intricacies of the subject-matter represent one side of this attempt, the determination to do everything possible in the way of grading and ordering the subject-matter the other.

The admission of an uncertainty principle means that never again can school science afford to be taught quite so positively as it has been in the past. Hence the tendency to transfer the onus from the teacher to the pupil. The importance attached to laboratory work, the provision of equipment and apparatus for first-hand usage, the sequencing of experiments so as to encourage the pupil to go it alone, the regular testing which enables him to check his own progress – all these must be seen as an attempt to convert an instruction-situation (lessons, demonstrations) into a learning-situation (investigations, inquiries). It is the difference between a closed system and an open-ended one. The one is characteristic of the teacher in the classroom, the other of the scientist in his laboratory.

This is not to say that the methods adopted by the teacher of science are identical with those of the research worker, only that the pupil's point of departure (i.e. not knowing what the outcome is to be) is very like that of a researcher. With this in mind, the new approach is more concerned to prepare the ground, provide materials and offer guidance than it is to dole out information. 'Learning is connecting', said Thorndike. By the same token it may be said that teaching is arranging.

REFERENCES

1 Addison Lee, 'Biology from 1890 to BSCS', Unpublished paper, Science Education Center, University of Texas
2 *The New School Science*, p. 53, American Association for the Advancement of Science
3 Ibid., pp. 42–43

Every revolution in poetry is apt to be, and sometimes to announce itself to be, a return to common speech. That is the revolution which Wordsworth announced in his prefaces and he was right; but the same revolution had been carried out a century before by Oldham, Waller, Denham and Dryden, and the same revolution was due again something over a century later.

T. S. Eliot *The Music of Poetry*

So here I am, in the middle way, having had twenty years . . .
Trying to learn the use of words, and every attempt
Is a wholly new start, and a different kind of failure
Because one has only learnt to get the better of words
For the thing one no longer has to say, or the way in which
One is no longer disposed to say it. And so each venture
Is a new beginning, a raid on the inarticulate
With shabby equipment always deteriorating
In the general mess of imprecision of feeling,
Undisciplined squads of emotion.

T. S. Eliot 'East Coker'

CHAPTER SIX

English at the Crossroads

Useless to ask whether you recall the first lesson you ever received in English: if it was not at the hands of the midwife it was at your mother's breast. From the miraculous birth of language, commencing with the squalls attending parturition, grows a whole network of accomplishments leading to articulate speech, which provides the springboard for the acquisition of the more formal, second-order symbolic skills of reading, writing, and rhetoric, which in turn lay the foundations (for some) of literary appreciation and criticism and (for all) of rational discourse. To call all these 'English', as we do, is excusable only so long as we remember that the term is multi-purposive.

'Every teacher a teacher of English', says the hoary maxim. But what is English if not a rag-bag stuffed full of ill-assorted bundles? Unlike other specialist subjects, the proper business of English studies ranges over issues which are as wide and deep as life itself, with the result that it often seems as if the teacher of English has no option but to take in other people's washing. While this is true at all stages of development, the multi-purpose nature of English teaching becomes increasingly problematical in the secondary school. So far as sixth-form studies are concerned, the current trend is described by Geoffrey Hoare in a passage which is worth quoting in full:

> What's done now isn't exactly new. Grammar, précis, comprehension, essay, Eng.Lit. by character and context – all these have a place. English teaching is still largely concerned with communication, with the art of writing (and, increasingly, saying) what you

mean; and of understanding what someone else meant. Recently, however, there has been a startling shift of emphasis. English is now seen as the principal academic channel of a boy's *moral* education. This means that during English lessons a boy learns with a new directness and seriousness about himself and the society in which he lives. Periods will be spent on, say, advertising, or TV or the film and other forms of pop culture and mass communication; or on the quality of life in cities, and town planning; or, perilously, on the work and influence of Freud, Adler and Jung. What were once red herrings become the main dish. It means, too, a rather different approach to literature. Books were once studied because they were 'acknowledged masterpieces' of importance in the history of English literature. The choice now falls on (sometimes lesser) works that deal with situations of concern to boys, written by men who are themselves concerned, or 'committed'. Gone, at school-level, are Addison and Steele, so much favoured a generation ago: in have come not only George Eliot and D. H. Lawrence but books like Hartley's *The Go-between*, Golding's *Lord of the Flies* and Salinger's *Catcher in the Rye*. It is not just a question of drawing parallels, of cerebral instruction and comment. It is important that a boy should be emotionally involved in what he reads; dragged, from the character and situation in the book, through the hedge backward to self-awareness; moved, in discussion and when he writes, to new insights about himself and those around him. The traditional scholarly, donnish approach gives way to new seriousness, *belles-lettres* to 'life', what is of historic importance to what is of contemporary significance, and, even more narrowly, of significance to the growing boy. What use a golden key if it doesn't fit the wards of the lock?

    This apparently innocent, laudable shift in English teaching slowly and sometimes imperfectly understood, has had effects which have aroused the strongest feelings of those on the staff who teach other subjects. There are some who complain that far too little time and care are now given to the simple mechanics of writing: 'never seem to have *heard* of punctuation'. Others are doubtful about so much concentration on the here and now: a proper understanding even of the present they urge is dependent on a historical sense, on being able to see books and their writers growing out of the differing, changing beliefs and views of different epochs. Moreover, this lack of a sense of historical relativity, this emphasis on what is contemporary,

significant to the boys, on self-awareness, is seen by many as disturb-
ingly self-centred, however high-minded. The English department
is seen by some as purveying criticisms of society, directly and
through the books chosen, but, for a lack of historical approach, not
providing a compensatory insight into how and why societies are as
they are. Idealistic adolescents finding our social forms and arrangements 'dishonest', discouraging to sincerity, care for others, concern
for truth, quickly slip, the critics feel, into an uncomprehending,
rebellious, anti-social individualism – a complex epitomised, say, in
the ban-the-bomb marches. Because the 'new' English teaching has
a 'life not *belles-lettres*' approach it is the focus of conflicting views of
how boys behave and how they should be guided to behave.

The English department, then, is seen as an unexpected group
chaplaincy, with masters' desks their pulpits and five or six periods
a week at their disposal with each form, at a time when official
divinity is reduced to one period a week and few boys go to church.[1]

But if English has to be thought of as a house of many mansions,
in which the teacher figures as a jack-of-all-trades, it is also a
house divided against itself. The division between those who live
in its two main wings is exemplified in the protracted and bitter
quarrels between philologists and men of letters prior to, and after,
the establishment of the Merton Professorship of English Language
and Literature at Oxford in 1885. In one camp, the 'Dilettanti
School' as their opponents called them, were scholars of the calibre
of Walter Raleigh, Edmund Gosse, John Morley, and Matthew
Arnold, upholders of the cause of purely literary studies; in the
other, the 'Saxonists', men like Joseph Wright, C. H. Firth, and
A. S. Napier (the first occupant of the chair), who championed the
claims of language as a discipline. For the one, any approach to
the teaching of English through grammar condemned itself as
'a wretched system of word-mongering and pedantry'. For the
other, the rooted objection to literature *per se* was expressed by
E. A. Freeman, one of the disappointed candidates:

Many people seem to think that any kind of study of which anything
can be said, any study which is found pleasing or profitable for anybody, should at once find its place in the University system, and

should be made at least an alternative subject for the B.A. examination. . . . It is surely allowable that some studies are undesirable because they are not solid enough, and others because they are in a certain sense too solid, that is because they are too purely technical. As subjects for the examination for the first degree, we do not want professional subjects – professional subjects, when fit for the University course at all, ought to come after – and we do not want, we will not say frivolous subjects, but subjects which are merely light, elegant, interesting. As subjects for examination we must have subjects in which it is possible to examine.[2]

Merely because the arguments and counter-arguments resorted to in this nineteenth-century parochial dispute now seem decidedly dated it should not be thought that the causes of disagreement have disappeared: on the contrary, they survive to this day and remain a source of friction in academic circles. So far as the undergraduate studies are concerned, the marriage of convenience between English language and literature has always been an uneasy affair, and one which some of the new foundations have been glad to dissolve; and at the secondary school level much the same conflict of opinion is reflected in the coolness – it can scarcely be called a controversy – between the evangelists of the 'new writing' and the advocates of the 'new grammar'. Even at the primary stage, where the aims are not so diffuse, teachers tend to fall into two classes: those who maintain that priority must be given to self-expression and that the child's imagination must be immunised against the misuses of language in an age of mass communication – and those who prefer to follow a more humdrum course which at least ensures that the pupil can write grammatically and spell correctly, in other words, keeping English as a subject 'which it is possible to examine'. The fact that differences in method between so-called 'creative English' and 'functional English' arise from different aims, and that they are in no sense antipathetic, is apparently incapable of bringing the two sides together.

To complicate matters there is a widespread distrust of language itself. For the poet, original writing nowadays cannot hope to be anything better than

> a raid on the inarticulate
> *With shabby equipment always deteriorating*
> *In the general mess of imprecision of feeling,*
> *Undisciplined squads of emotion.*

For the thinker, likewise, unremitting attention to the pitfalls inherent in the use of words has come to be so obsessive that in recent decades practically the whole of philosophy has been taken up with linguistic analysis. In this predicament, artist, scientist, and teenager take refuge in the semi-private language of their respective peer-groups.

All this is symptomatic of social disharmony and cultural crisis.

> Nor is it difficult to see why this is so. While Hegel's dictum that 'language is the actuality of culture' may be an overstatement, it is certainly true that language embodies not only the categories and terms in which thought is carried on but also the attitudes, habits, standards and ideas of the social group. Hence, as Urban observes, to question the validity of language is in a very real sense to question the validity of the culture itself. The emergence of semantics, therefore, as a major problem is significant evidence of loss of communication and integration. A widespread feeling that the words traditionally used to express ethical ideas are empty and meaningless jargon to be employed, if at all, only in a ritual sense is an almost certain indication that moral understanding and communication has been seriously disrupted.[3]

Language is most stable in isolated communities – witness the durability of Icelandic or Sardinian down the centuries. But in the modern world the isolated community is an anachronism. The 'well of English undefiled' has become a cosmopolitan reservoir in which English English, Scottish English, American English, Indian English and effluents from every country under the sun are blended. The same process affects the jealously guarded purity of the French language – and all the efforts of the ah-the-past-masters of the Académie Française, Mongénéral and *Le Monde* are likely to be of no avail against the inroads of franglais.

There is a further complication. Thanks to the tremendous power of mass media, television in particular, the centre of interest is shifting from the written to the spoken word. This shift from literacy (which in post-Renaissance times has implied certain standards of proficiency in reading and writing) to oracy (which places the accent on listening and saying) is perhaps more obviously visible in the teaching of foreign languages, but it affects the teaching of English no less markedly and subtly. In doing so, unfortunately, it aggravates the problem of 'bilingualism' which many teachers of English had always had to face. The conflict which arises in the minds of pupils for whom the usage and idioms of the classroom are not the same as those current in the playground or the home is likely to be accentuated if there is a clash between methods aiming at oral proficiency and methods which aim at literacy as it has been understood hitherto.

In Britain, that is. In America, even in places where Quintilian has never been heard of, the affinities with the ancient Roman way of life have led to a different persuasion.

> Speechifying is not for them the pastime of the leisure moment. It plays a central part in the academic curriculum. Every campus has its quota of speech professors or directors of forensics. . . . The ability to argue clearly on one's feet is likely to be as essential to anyone as the ability to argue on paper, and in some professions, those of teacher, lawyer, politician, churchman, television pundit or teenage satirist, possibly more. Both the techniques of delivery and of the presentation of content come within the scope of a course in speech. This is not the place to describe or prescribe the nature of such a syllabus; we wish only to say that in our opinion of all the subjects that we found taught in America, but ignored in England, the study of the spoken word in all its aspects seems to us to be the one that most demands imitation.[4]

As to that, there will no doubt be other opinions. Still, the trend exists; and the extent to which trans-Atlantic influences are responsible for it provides a nice topic for cross-cultural investigation.

In fact, many of the techniques applied in the language-laboratory, for example, have developed as by-products of the analysis of languages like Choctaw and Kwakiutl for which no grammar or dictionary was available – and which had virtually no literature. These techniques, which stress the importance of an oral, conversational approach to language learning, have been aided and abetted by technological developments which, however indirectly, have had the effect of making some of the traditional scholastic skills – handwriting for one – seem almost obsolete. Moreover, linguists themselves have become more interested in grammars which are descriptive of the language as it is actually spoken than in prescriptive grammars, at any rate those based on literate (Latinized) concepts of formal correctness.

Now while it may be true that grammar is the logic of speech just as logic is the grammar of reason, the rules of literacy are not necessarily the same as those of oracy. In the written language, as Pei points out, there are two possibilities: it may follow the spoken language, symbolizing its sounds, or it may avoid any such connexion altogether.

As he says,

> In their anxiety to restrict language to a pattern of sounds too many linguists have forgotten that the sound symbols of the spoken tongue are neither more nor less symbolical of human thought and meaning than the various forms of activity – gestural, pictorial, ideographic, even artistic – by which men have conveyed significant messages to one another since the dawn of history.[6]

Among other things, the fact that English script is notorious for being only partly phonetic helps to explain why methods of teaching reading are so varied, not to say chaotic. One is left wondering, indeed, why the proponents of alphabetic and phonic methods have not long since called a truce on this simple fact instead of asserting as adamantly as some of them have done that all the good arguments are on one side and none on the other. The conclusion can only be that throughout the ages children have somehow or other contrived to learn how to read in spite of the methods used rather than because of them.* Certainly, if the

---

* i.t.a. (Initial Teaching Alphabet).
Attempted reforms in English orthography have a long history, culminating in the abortive Simplified Spelling Bill of 1953. Experiments during the

choice is to be between old-fashioned 'look and say' and some of the latest concoctions of the linguists, the verdict is likely to go against the latter: for what, in the name of enlightened teaching, is the infants' mistress to make of a reader which kicks off on page 1 with such gibberish as:

---

nineteenth century with phonetic spelling, initiated by Sir Isaac Pitman, provided the latter's grandson, Sir James Pitman, with the basis for his Augmented Roman Alphabet, now generally referred to as the Initial Teaching Alphabet, Its adoption in infants' classes, now widespread in the UK and also in the USA. has aroused conflicting claims and counter-claims. Sir Edward Boyle, as Minister of Education, spoke of 'these exciting and interesting developments'. The London Institute of Education and the National Foundation for Educational Research are at present conducting a wide-scale investigation of the results of using these new reading materials. Possibly the most enthusiastic (and the least cautious!) of the accounts of experiments with i.t.a. offered to date is that of Maurice Harrison, Director of Education for Oldham: *Instant Reading: The Story of the Initial Teaching Alphabet* (Pitman, 1964).

According to Harrison, 'The new approach is not a teaching method: it is merely a simplification of the medium, of the early material with which the child is required to deal. He learns and puts to use 45 characters instead of more than 2,000 characterizations and he has to learn only these 45 signs in the greatly simplified code. That is the sum and the substance of the i.t.a. approach. Only when he has learnt to do that simpler task does he tackle the complexities of normal spelling. Methods of using this simplified medium will vary and different teachers will find themselves apter with some methods than with others. . . . The fact remains that the least successful teachers are more successful than they used to be – and apparently more successful in this particular job of teaching reading than the very best teachers using the old medium'. (*Op. cit.*, p. 186.)

Until firm research findings are forthcoming the fact remains that educationists cannot afford to be quite so dogmatic. Present indications are that young children enjoy the new approach, that for many the reading process is facilitated by the removal of the quirks in conventional spelling, and that the transfer at a later stage to normal reading material is accomplished smoothly. For a more sober appraisal of the possibilities of i.t.a. see Hunter Diack's *In Spite of the Alphabet* (Chatto and Windus, 1965, pp. 156–76), where the suggestion is that the reading achievement of infants in i.t.a. experimental groups actually compares unfavourably with the achievement of pupils taught by the 'phonic words method'.

Information about i.t.a. is distributed by the Initial Teaching Alphabet Foundation, 9, Southampton Place, London, W.C.1.

Dan can fan Nan.
Nan, fan Dan.
Dan, fan Nan.
Dan ran a van.
Dan ran a tan van.
A man ran a tan van . . .

or

A CAT BATS AT A RAT
CATS BAT AT RATS?

As Hunter Diack remarks, the linguist 'is stretching optimism to the limit if he expects a scheme of teaching that has so much of the early nineteenth century about it to be accepted in a world where the reading material for children is expected to be meaningful and interesting.'[5]

Regardless of the level, it is never an either-or choice between literacy and oracy with which the English teacher is presented: truer to say that it is always a case of all or nothing. No one doubts that the ability to comprehend passages of prose and poetry has to be cultivated, that the pupil's ability to express himself coherently in speech as well as in writing is a *sine qua non*. Where doubt sets in is over the question of where the emphasis should be placed – and the emphasis, as we have seen, is shifting all the time. So that while it may be the case that oral, conversational aims have to some extent supplanted the old reading and writing objectives in the teaching of English, as they have in the teaching of foreign languages, and that the traditional models of grammar and literature look like being replaced, it is still far from clear what the new objectives and the new models are to be. Whereas it is perfectly legitimate to speak of a new mathematics or a new approach to the teaching of science, the 'new English' remains inchoate. School textbooks on syntax based on Chomsky's transformational grammar are already on sale in the USA and courses dealing with the 'new rhetoric' well in hand, but in this country it seems that the linguists are not ready to go into action (although there are persistent rumours that they are about to do so) and that the counsel for oracy is biding its time. In brief, the situation can only be characterized as a general mess of imprecision, befogged by all kinds of unanswered (and unasked) questions. For what purposes and at what stages is an oral approach necessarily the best, or even desirable? What is the relative importance of the skills of listening, speaking, reading, and writing, and how is a balance to be struck between them? How can each of them be most effectively developed? Is it true that the child learns language one way, adults another? If so, is it a weakness of the oral approach that it makes no allowance for this difference? Must the formal study of grammar wait upon the learner's power of generalization, and if so, how, if at all, is grammar to be taught at the primary stage?

But if the situation is confused it is also pregnant with possibilities. While it is not possible to draw up a critical-path analysis of the future of English teaching, innovations in the schools indicate that its course will be along two main lines.

THE 'NEW WRITING'

Complaints about 'word-mongering and pedantry' have been aired in and out of schools for many a long day. Too often the pupil's written work has been a joyless ink-exercise. Sentence formation as a logical step-by-step development, using mechanical formulae, is felt by many teachers to be the wrong approach to 'composition', blighting any originality the pupil might have. Insistence on correct spelling and punctuation have proved more of a bugbear than a help just as insistence on correct perspective once proved a bugbear in the teaching of child art. Even when the child had something to say (which was by no means always) his expression was fettered by the need to observe the letter of the law, and when it broke free of its fetters and became spontaneous he was penalized.

One of the most moving examples of the way in which the young author's creativity is stifled is quoted by John Blackie in *Good Enough for The Children?*. A class of nine-year-olds were set to write a composition on the subject of 'My father'. One boy asked whether he might be allowed to write about his *real* father. This is what he wrote:

> My father is on the broad side and tall side. My father was a hard working man and he had a lot of money. He was not fat or thin. . . . His age was about 30 years when he died, he had a good reputation, he is a married man. When he was in hospital I went to see him every Sunday afternoon. I asked him how he was going on, he told me he was getting a lot better. My father was very kind to me and gave me and my cousins cigarette cards. He likes doing woodwork, my father, for me, and he likes a little game of cards now and then; or a game of darts. He chops the wood and saws the planks and he is a handsome man but he is dead. He worked at the rubber works before he died.

Says Blackie, 'The comment that the teacher had thought fit to write at the foot of this intensely moving and, in its way, beautiful piece of writing, was: "Tenses. You keep mixing past and present." '[7]

Let the Children Write, The Excitement of Writing, Education through English, English for the Rejected, The Eye of Innocence – children and their poetry – these are some of the book titles which proclaim the growing revolt (or should it be revulsion?) against this barren state of affairs. Common to them all is the conviction that the child's use of language deserves to be respected in the same way that his use of line and colour has been in art teaching. Free-writing, creative writing, intensive writing, new writing – call it what you will – still lacks a convincing rationale to match the convictions which inspire it, but essentially it represents the intro-duction into the classroom, two generations later, of the same methods that revolutionized child art. Some of these have been rightly criticized as suffering from the same faults, unlimited free-expression for one, as did the teaching of art at one stage. They have been derided, not always without justification, as owing more to therapy than to sound pedagogy, a classroom version of the free-association techniques employed in psycho-analysis. Children are being weaned away from Georgian styles of prose and poetry and freed for Joyce and Eliot at a time when they cannot even write a decent letter, it is complained.

To allow the learner to become completely absorbed in painting is one thing, quite another to let him splash around with words, say the objectors: the imagery-of-the-innocent-eye argument may hold good for art but it is misapplied when it comes to the craft of writing.

In fairness it has to be said that some of the eulogists of intensive writing have done their cause a disservice by reading more into the children's efforts than the graffiti warranted. Sloppy thinking and extravagant claims are calculated to deter rather than attract the approval of teachers on the look-out for an imaginative approach. If the following are taken as typical specimens, the 'new writing' is liable to be laughed out of court before it gets going in earnest:

> Here is some more (about the donkey in the lion's skin):
>
> > 'So he went to a fled and hed behind a bash and he roaed like a loin and the lumsy cows went limbering to the other side of the fled. Then he went to the framyard and hid behind the sebles and roaed like a loin and the geres gacled and the ducks gact and the dog bardt and theywas sush a nose that the farmer woke up from his nap'
>
> Gorgeous! The child's expression outstrips her spelling powers, but she will put that right later as courageously as she tries new words now. Read it like *Finnegans Wake* and forget all the tedious spelling fuss, and what a lovely perception it shows! What a sensitive mind that creates these key phrases, telling phrases with their own rhythm. . . . Kate has never read Chaucer, but she is kneeling to the same daisy of life as that great Master did.[8]

Or consider the case of Joan Stall:

> (IQ76. Accompanied on her primary school record with the phrase, 'Has no originality or imagination'.)
>
> In answer to the phrase of condemnation let us quote from Joan's examination paper at the end of her first school year with me:

A poem

A little yellow bird sat on my window sill
He hop and poped about
He wisheld he cherped
I trid to chach my little yellow brid
but he flew into the golden yellow sun,
O how I wish that was my yellow brid.

Do we not hear William Blake faintly in the background?[9]

We do not. Instead, we hear distinct overtones, pretty garbled ones at that, of a pop song which reached the Top Twenty just about the time this ingenuous little effusion was penned. On this evidence, who is to say that the assessment of the school record card was altogether wrong? And who shall blame us if we think that the ultimate absurdity has been reached when we are told that, in the event, 'Joan became, as it were, the Ivy Compton-Burnett of the class'?

Such passages are fair game for satire. The pity of it is that behind the pretentious mystique which surrounds it, the 'new writing' vogue stands for principles which are not to be disparaged. Easy enough to pooh-pooh some of the methods used to evoke images, thoughts and feelings as no better than a return to the old object lesson - producing a mackerel or a skull or some other quaint museum-piece and asking the children to jot down the first things that come into their heads. At least let it be said that the results are no worse, and often a great deal better, than those obtained in the past. There is, come to think of it, a striking resemblance between these open-ended invitations to writing and those now being tried out in the teaching of science – the mackerel and the skull serving in lieu of the black box and the unidentified object in the Chemical Bond Approach and the candle flame in CHEM Study. Either way, there is unquestionably an infusion of zest which must be applauded, and a release of creative impulses which is heartening. The latest anthologies of children's written work speak for themselves. Significantly, some of the choicest examples come from primary schools and from pupils

whose scholastic achievements are otherwise decidely modest. In
the field of educational innovations this is as promising a sector as
any. If only those who toil in it would stop kneeling at the daisies!

THE 'NEW LINGUISTICS'

Unchivalrous as it would be to Margaret Langdon, Sybil Marshall,
Eva Langholm *et al* to infer that the 'new writing' movement
represents the womanish side of English teaching, the side which
appeals to sentiment and intuition, and that the 'new linguistics'
stands for the masculine side, the one which appeals to more
strictly rational procedures, it is nevertheless a fact that the former
has shown itself to be most successful at the primary stage whereas
the latter's contribution looks like being most helpful at the secondary stage. Be this as it may, there is undeniably a difference
between creative and functional English. This is where the rift
between 'literature' and 'language' begins – and the rift remains.

It has been apparent for some considerable time that the kind
of grammar taught in most schools is largely unproductive. Many
teachers and many pupils have been left with the impression that
going through the motions of parsing and analysis – which is what
it amounted to in practice – is a rather pointless exercise, utterly
divorced from normal English usage. As a consequence there
has been a growing tendency to think that the practice is more
honoured in the breach than the observance. From sheer inanition
and for want of obvious relevance, the teaching of formal
grammar has receded further and further into the background.

But if traditional grammar has been exposed as threadbare it is
not as yet certain how a new one is to be tailored. Typical of the
gnawing uncertainty which afflicts many teachers is the 1965
memorandum, *The Primary School*, issued by the Scottish Education
Department, which recommends that 'grammar should not be
taught at all under that name in the earlier years of the primary
school', only to add somewhat lamely – 'that does not mean
that grammar is not in fact taught'. Until a definite lead is forthcoming from the linguists it seems that questions about what is to

be taught and how it is to be taught will continue to go by default.

Far from presenting a united front, unfortunately, linguistic scholars, like philosophers and psychologists (only more so, if anything), arrange themselves in contending factions: the Traditionalists (for whom Jespersen is still the last word), the Structuralists, the Neo-Firthians in Britain and, in the USA, the Transformationalists (for whom Noam Chomsky is a quasi-religious leader). As a class, they tend to give the impression of being somewhat withdrawn, inhabiting a stratospheric world of their own, far removed from the mundane problems of the schools. To the neophyte, their writings are bleakly forbidding, couched in a highly esoteric terminology which is often difficult to follow. In this they resemble the mathematicians. The comparison is indeed apt for it is only within the last decade that theoretic linguistics has emerged from the privacy of 'pure' research. Previously it was a neglected field and those engaged in it were few and far between. Thanks to their efforts, the laborious task of building up a detailed and accurate description of the native language is now nearing completion so that we are at last beginning to get a clear picture of how English works. The discovery that theoretic research has practical uses, for example, in the teaching of English as a foreign language, in communication engineering and the design of translating machines, has provided the motive (and the finance!) that was previously lacking in applied linguistics. The arrival of applied linguistics is timely, coinciding as it does with the revival of interest in the teaching of English as a language and the increased attention now being paid to the spoken word.

This advance took place in a fairly short period of time, largely between 1945 and 1950 as far as British-based teaching of English is concerned. Since that time, 'English teaching' has very largely evolved into 'English-language teaching', and for several years further developments have consisted mainly in improvements in classroom techniques and materials. It seems to us that the profession is now ripe for yet another big advance; it is largely since 1950 –

that is to say, since the change towards practical teaching – that the main developments in linguistics have taken place in Britain, and it is only since 1955 that the relevance of linguistics to language teaching has been properly considered here.[10]

Closing the gap between advanced theory and everyday practice is not going to be easy even with the services of an adequate supply of applied linguists as middlemen. Eventually, but not before the colleges of education and university departments of education revise their courses of teacher-training, it may well be that we shall see a new kind of English specialist, one who is qualified first and foremost as a master of native language skills – and that in the early stages at least his appearance on the scene will probably be resented by some of his Eng.Lit. colleagues. Obviously, it is going to take time for the ideas of the linguists to seep down to the classroom level – much longer than it has taken the new mathematics, for instance – and even when this happens the indications are that these ideas will prove most fruitful with senior pupils, and then only with competent teachers.

At the moment, textbooks expounding the new grammar and lexis are still in the process of being written, if in fact their authors have got so far as committing their thoughts to paper at all. This is perhaps not entirely regrettable. In the USA a number of textbooks based on Chomsky's transformational grammar are already on the market, but quite apart from the inherent limitations in the Chomsky model conditions of English teaching in this country are so different from those prevailing in American high schools as to make it unlikely that the adoption of a trans-Atlantic model is desirable.

Transformational grammar may be broadly defined as an attempt to restore grammar to its rightful place in the mind (i.e. as a human construct) using the methods of symbolic logic. It takes the 'kernel sentence' as its unit and starting-point and develops a twin set of rules from which, in theory, all possible sentence-formations can be derived. Among the principal objections levelled against it by Professor M. A. K. Halliday and his associates is the fact that it makes no allowance for relationships *between* sentences, and that it virtually ignores the actual *situations* in which language is used (context, register, etc).

This is not the place to enter into a detailed discussion of the pros and cons of 'Chomskyite' and 'Hallidayan' grammars – the differences between the American and British schools of thought are not so enormous that they cannot be resolved, and judging by their latest pronouncements, look like being resolved in the near future. Enough to say that when it becomes available the new grammar will differ from the old in a number of important respects. In the first place, it will be more *systematic*: between them, grammar and lexis will define the finite number of meaningful choices which produce the infinite permutations and combinations of speech and writing. In the case of grammar, where the choice is narrowly restricted, the learner will see the rules of the game as a closed system: in the case of lexis, where the range of choice is wider, as an open set. In the second place, the new grammar will be *productive*, i.e. more readily applicable to the mastery of language-skills. It will also be more *powerful*, if only because it possesses a higher degree of generality.

To begin with, needless to say, its notation will be unfamiliar. Before the rank and file of teachers become *au fait* with it they will need to unlearn many of their stock notions and shed some of their vested interests. In any case, it would be premature to claim that applied linguistics is ready for the job which is waiting to be done. Theoretic linguistics still has a fair way to go, apparently!

'Provided the theory is valid, comprehensive and consistently applied, *but not otherwise*, we can make statements about the grammar of a language which apply to vast numbers of different actual speech events, and are therefore of great value to the learner of the language: they provide source material for what the textbook and the teacher have to tell him.'[11] As already indicated, this essential source-material is still in the process of being prepared.

In the meantime we must be grateful for such a book as *The Linguistic Sciences and Language Teaching* which charts the way ahead and outlines a framework of organization for language teaching which relates linguistic theory to pedagogical principles.

Its exposition of 'methodics', to which the reader is referred, is uncannily like those who have emerged from the curriculum study projects in mathematics and the sciences, and it has obvious affinities with the techniques of programmed learning examined in the next chapter. In each case, there is the same preoccupation with the need for carefully defined objectives, with the analysis of structure and with the staging of courses and the sequencing of instruction. No clearer résumé of the rationale behind the teaching of English has yet been given, and no fuller or more convincing statement of the kind of prescriptive theory of instruction discussed in the final chapter of *The Teaching Revolution* has yet appeared.

What is English if not a rag-bag stuffed full of ill-assorted bundles?, we asked earlier on. This is certainly not the way the authors of *The Linguistic Sciences and Language Teaching* look at the question. Instead, they categorize the subject under the headings of *substance* (noises, marks on paper, etc), *form* (grammar and lexis), and *situation* (social purpose). This enables them to draw up a preliminary framework within which the structure of English language can be envisaged:

SUBJECT CONCERNED	PHONETICS		LINGUISTICS		
LEVEL (*general*)	Substance *phonic or graphic*	*relation of form and substance*	Form	Context *relation of form and situation*	Situation *non-linguistic phenomena*
LEVEL (*specific*)	Phonetics Script	Phonology Graphology *writing system*	Grammar *and* Lexis *vocabulary*	Semantics	

Having done this, the next step is to see what is involved in the various levels of language-skills, which are tabulated as follows:

GRAPHOLOGY	PHONOLOGY	FORM (*Grammar*)	FORM (*Lexis*)
Paragraph Orthographic sentence		Sentence	
Sub-sentence	Tone group Foot Syllable	Clause Group	
Orthographic word Letter	Phoneme	Word Morpheme	Lexical item

Next to be considered are the interrelations between the various language-skills, their order of appearance and what the task analysis experts call the 'subordinate capabilities' required for their acquisition. The relation between language-skills and the introduction of items (i.e. instruction) at different levels of language is then tabulated thus:

	CATEGORIES OF LANGUAGE				
LANGUAGE-SKILLS	GRAMMAR 'Structures' 'Grammatical patterns'	LEXIS 'Vocabulary'	CONTEXT 'Situations'	PHONOLOGY 'Patterns of sound'	GRAPHOLOGY 'System of writing and spelling'
1. UNDERSTANDING SPEECH			Dependent on what has been introduced in the preceding column; all items in grammar and lexis must be fully understood from the outset; new items must be introduced in meaningful ('contextual') ways	Full range essential from the outset	Not essential
2. SPEAKING	Some grammatical and lexical items are needed from the outset; they can be increased progressively				
3. READING					
4. WRITING				Not essential but often helpful	Full range essential from the outset

Finally, a summary of the framework of the procedures to be

followed by the teacher of English ('methodics'), including [1] definition of objectives, [2] organization of courses, [3] sequencing of instruction, and [4] testing, is presented:

PROCEDURES OF METHODICS	LEVELS OF LANGUAGE AND THEIR EQUIVALENTS IN METHODOLOGY			
	PHONOLOGY 'sounds of speech'	GRAMMAR 'structures' 'grammatical patterns'	LEXIS 'vocabulary'	CONTEXT 'situations'
LIMITATION *Restriction* *Selection*				
GRADING *Staging* *Sequencing*				
PRESENTATION *Initial teaching* *Repeated teaching*				
TESTING *Formal/Informal* *Objective/Subjective* *Tests/Examinations*				

Even if the reader gathers little or nothing from an inspection of their bald outlines, no excuse needs to be offered for reproducing these four tables.[12] However sketchily, they illustrate an approach to English teaching which is visibly like those now being tried out in other subjects, and they exemplify features common to the innovative movement as a whole.

It would be wrong to conclude from all this that English as a school subject is to be reinterpreted as 'English language' exclusively. As the authors of *The Linguistic Sciences and Language Teaching* point out:

> It is sometimes assumed that linguists are simply advocating the use of linguistics as such in the school classroom; but this is not the case. Replacing good teachers with no linguistic knowledge or training by teachers trained in linguistics does not in itself make much difference to the effectiveness of the language teaching taking place in their classes. It has been tried, of course; in the early days of the linguistic renaissance many people, especially in the United States, thought

that linguistics could be given a direct classroom role, just as many people in Britain once thought, and perhaps still do think, that in the teaching of modern languages the science of phonetics could be given a direct classroom role. In fact, the place for both phonetics and linguistics is *behind* the classroom teacher, in the training that he received for his job as a teacher, in the preparation of the syllabus according to which his teaching programme is organized, and in the preparation of the teaching materials of all kinds that he makes use of in class. These are the points at which the linguistic sciences affect language teaching.[13]

Very soon now, it may be hoped, these new materials will be finding their way into the schools. As it is, a revised version of traditional grammar is being adopted here and there with encouraging results. As happened when set theory was first introduced in the new mathematics syllabus, the response from the pupils has been heartening. Teachers who are sometimes hard put to tell the difference between a phoneme and a morpheme are often agreeably surprised by the readiness of eight-, nine-, and ten-year-olds to grasp the significant relationships between verbal symbols. If learning the parts of speech was a bore for most children, many (and not only the abler ones) find it intriguing to discover the hierarchical structure implied in the morpheme–word–group–clause–sentence series as exemplified by the letters 's–t–o–p' in

'The car is stopping'	(*Morpheme*)
'The car won't stop'	(*Word*)
'All cars stop here'	(*Group*)
'Stop or I shoot!'	(*Clause*)
'Stop!'	(*Sentence*)

It may be that a Hawthorn effect has to be allowed for in some of these latest ventures and that the dullness which has always dogged the teaching of grammar will sooner or later descend upon them. This is possible, but all things considered it seems improbable (just as it seems improbable that the new grammar, when it materializes, will provide an infallible, foolproof formula which

K

will guarantee high standards of functional English for all pupils). Without looking too far ahead, however, it seems safe to say that besides being more systematic, the new approach will be more intrinsically interesting and capable of opening up a wider range of language studies than has been available to pupils hitherto. Methods of teaching will be no less open-ended and investigative than those which characterize the 'new writing' or the new mathematics.

In theory, the new grammar may appear to be infernally difficult, too abstruse for tender minds. In practice it turns out to be a good deal more illuminating than the old ever was. Instead of treating the parts of the speech as discrete units, it explains the functions of words in terms of their contextual signals. Thus, whereas as the old method was content to classify 'eager' and 'easy' as adjectives and to inform children that both were 'describing words', the new is more concerned to show how the positioning of a word affects the shape and meaning of the sentence as a whole, as in

John is easy to please
John is eager to please.

In less formal ways, too, the growing tendency is for the usual 'comprehension' exercises so beloved by the English teacher in the past (and so well hated by his pupils) to be replaced by the study of passages of prose in different registers – advertising copy, newspaper editorials, radio and television scripts, legal documents, the Bible, sports commentaries, etc, so that pupils can become acquainted with the styles of utterance and writing appropriate to a wide variety of usages. Even shock tactics in problem-solving may be resorted to, as happens when pupils are presented with passages in an unknown foreign language (or even an invented one) and asked to decipher their potential meaning as best they can – reminiscent of the black-box-and-the-unidentified-object experiment in the Chemical Bond Approach. Playbacks of recorded conversations, discussions, monologues, play readings and even playground hubbub provide their own opportunities for making children language-conscious.

Linguistics as the scholar understands it may be a highly rigorous discipline, but as more and more teachers are finding it has its Stage of Romance and can easily be made fascinating. How soon it will lead on to the Stage of Precision, and in doing so satisfy the malcontents who protest that standards of functional English are deplorably low, can only be conjectured. The New Writing and the New Grammar may be the pillars of fire through which the teaching of English has to pass in order to reach the promised land – but Moses has yet to appear.

REFERENCES

1 Bob White et al. *Experiments in Education at Sevenoaks*, pp. 88–89 Constable Young Books, 1965
2 D. J. Palmer *The Rise of English Studies*, p. 99, Oxford University Press, 1965
3 W. O. Stanley *Education and Social Integration*, p. 50, Teachers College, Columbia, 1953
4 Jonathan Aitken and Michael Beloff *A Short Walk on the Campus*, pp. 15–16, Secker and Warburg, 1966
5 Mario Pei *The Story of Language*, p. 8, Mentor, 1949
6 Hunter Diack *In Spite of the Alphabet*, p. 155, Chatto and Windus, 1965
7 John Blackie *Good Enough for the Children?*, p. 16, Faber, 1963
8 David Holbrook *The Secret Places*, p. 216, Methuen, 1964
9 David Holbrook *English for the Rejected*, p. 54, Cambridge University Press, 1964
10 M. A. K. Halliday, Angus McIntosh, and Peter Strevens *The Linguistic Sciences and Language Teaching*, p. 185, Longmans, 1964
11 Ibid., p. 31
12 Ibid., pp. 18, 51, 209, and 222 respectively
13 Ibid., p. 187

THE CARPENTRY REVOLUTION
A Fable by W. A. Deterline

Once upon a time carpentry was a very frustrating business which depended on tools that rarely produced products of consistent quality. Carpenters labored hard with what they had, but their products were accepted only because there seemed to be no possibility of doing any better. Then one day a man who was not even a carpenter invented a tool he called a 'plane' and he suggested that carpenters could use it to great advantage in their work. No one listened to this man, of course. Some years later another who was not a carpenter either, invented a device he called a 'saw' and he made quite a bit of noise about his device and its potential in the carpentry business. Another man (also non-union) at about the same time invented a 'hammer' and he too made noise that attracted attention. Each of the three men attracted followers, some of whom were cooks and hunters and golf pros. Then a peculiar thing happened. Instead of providing a useful set of tools for the carpenters, the 'saws' and the 'planes' and the 'hammers' argued among themselves over which tool was best. The 'saws' said, 'Our tool works better on wood than a hammer or a plane', and the hammers said, 'Our tool hits nails and thumbs better than a saw or a plane', and the planes, well you know what they said. Then other voices were heard extolling the virtues of screw drivers, rasps, drills and all manner of other strange tools and furious controversies were waged over the question of who had the one tool that would solve all the carpenter's problems. A few unawares types tried using combinations of several tools, but they were quickly hooted out of town for their lack of imagination. The carpenters waited and waited for the dust to settle so that they could welcome the winner with a ticker-tape parade, but lost patience as the bickering continued and finally just shrugged shoulders and went back to work. Since everybody in the new tool missionary profession was so involved in his own little sphere of interest, the whole business finally collapsed. The cooks went back to cooking; the hunters went back to hunting: silence fell in the land. Several centuries later someone stumbled on to the records of the old controversies. After laughing at the silliness and futility of it all, he put together a highly flexible and effective tool kit that made carpentry the science it is today. Then many people lived happily ever after some of the time.

MORAL

Our classrooms could have had comfortable seats sooner if someone had kept his eyes on the ends not the means.

From *Trends in Programmed Instruction*, edited by G. D. Ofiesh and W. C. Meierhenry, Department of Audiovisual Instruction, National Education Association and the National Society for Programmed Instruction, 1964.

CHAPTER SEVEN

From Audio-visual Aids to Multi-media Communication Systems

For the teacher with ideals few experiences can be quite so disenchanting as to be left in charge of a coach-load of ten-year-olds touring a foreign country. A sunset over Monte Rosa and the chime of Alpine cow-bells, it seems, mean nothing to these young philistines: their eyes remained glued to tatty old comics, their ears attuned to the bleat and blare of pop songs from portable radio sets. As for the landscape, they have seen it often enough before in the cinema, in the colour supplements or at home on the telly: it interests them no more than does the backdrop to a Western film. They are the products of the age of the mass media, its victims, rather – for apparently they are so glutted with vicarious experience that, when it comes, first-hand acquaintance with the world around them turns out to be stale, flat, and unprofitable. In despondent mood, the teacher may well be reminded of the verdict which Pestalozzi pronounced upon the schoolchildren of his day – *Sie kennen wiel und wissen nichts.*

It is unwise to continue in this vein. To do so would mean adopting the stance of the literary intellectual whose vice has always been that of professing to 'view with alarm' and to 'feel concerned about' any developments which fall outside the enclave of high culture. Failure to come to terms with the mass media is a symptom of tradition-bound thinking which is all-too prevalent.

	Sensory Channel	Verbal or Pictorial?	Who Controls Rate and Repetition?	For Group or Individual Instruction?	Dating From	Availability in UK
MEDIEVAL						
Chalk, blackboard	Sight-Sound	Both	Maker	Group	Earliest times	All schools
Models, Charts, Maps, etc.	Sight	Chiefly pictorial	User	Either	Earliest times	All schools
RENAISSANCE						
Books	Sight	Chiefly verbal	User	Either	16th C.	All schools
FIRST INDUSTRIAL REVOLUTION						
Photographs, slides, film-strips	Sight	Pictorial	User	Group	Late 19th C.	All schools
Silent motion films	Sight	Pictorial	Maker	Group	Early 20th C.	Nearly all schools
Recordings	Sound	Verbal and Musical	Maker	Either	Early 20th C.	Nearly all schools
Radio (School Broadcasting)	Sound	Chiefly verbal	Maker	Either	1920s	Nearly all schools
Sound motion films	Sight-Sound	Both	Maker	Group	1930s	Nearly all schools
Television	Sight-Sound	Both	Maker	Either	1950s	Many schools
SECOND INDUSTRIAL REVOLUTION						
Tape recorders	Sound	Chiefly verbal	User	Either	1950s	Many schools
Language-laboratories	Sound	Verbal	User	Either	1950s	Few schools
Programmed Texts	Sight	Chiefly verbal	User	Individual	1950s	Few schools
Teaching Machines	Sight	Chiefly verbal	User	Individual	1950s	Very few schools
Closed-circuit Television	Sight-Sound	Both	User	Group	1960s	Very few schools
Computer-based Adaptive Teaching Machines	Sight-Sound	Both	User?	Either	?	Experimental

FIG 6 Time chart of mechanical devices used in teaching

Reproduced with amendments from *Four Generations of Educational Media in the USA* by Wilbur Schramm (Educational Studies and

Even so, teachers who have watched the steady proliferation of audio-visual aids in the classroom over the years may be forgiven for thinking that, on the whole, they have scarcely justified the high hopes placed in them. In view of the mounting expenditure on equipment, the time and trouble spent in handling it, and the problem of fitting it into the day-to-day work of the school, the Cassandras of the profession are entitled to ask whether the game is worth the candle. By definition, an *aid* is an adjunct to the craft of teaching. But in every case, while supplementing the teacher's work, the aid does nothing to simplify it. Whatever form it takes – school broadcast, television programme, film, or film-strip – the aid brings into the classroom a wealth of experience which cannot be conveyed half so vividly, if at all, either by word of mouth or by any other means. In doing so, the aid helps to make the teacher's presentation more stimulating, more meaningful, yes, but certainly not easier. Add to this the fact that, time and again, research studies report no significant differences between the scholastic attainments of pupils taught with and without the use of audio-visual aids, and it may be agreed that there is ground for scepticism.

Such scepticism is inevitable seeing that audio-visual aids represent, at best, a kind of half-way-house stage of development in a process which will eventually convert the teacher's craft into a technology. A glance at the accompanying diagram (reproduced from the author's *Teachers and Machines*) illustrates the point. At the risk of short-circuiting an argument which is bound to be long and involved, what has happened so far is that the provision of sophisticated instruments of communication has not been matched by an equally sophisticated theory of pedagogy. In other words, we have a technology of machines but as yet no adequate technology of instruction to go with it. For want of this, school television is left playing around with so-called 'enrichment' programmes, and even school broadcasting (in which the BBC may fairly be said to have set an example to the rest of the world) has made less impact than it might have during the forty years of its existence. The same is true of film. As Gagné remarks,

With such a combination of talents, the sound-motion picture should be a truly marvelous instrument for instruction! Unfortunately, the sound film that exploits these potentialities to their full extent is a great rarity. To a considerable degree, the reason may be that the content and sequencing of such films are governed by production considerations borrowed from the field of theatrical motion pictures. Except for highly specialized subjects (such as knot tying, micrometer reading), it is probably fair to say that a sound-motion-picture film that systematically uses the various instructional functions of moving pictures and oral communication in their proper places has yet to be made.[1]

So far as the purposes of formal education are concerned, the possibilities opened up by modern instrumentation have not, as a rule, been well enough understood to allow of their being fully exploited in common usage. The sole exception, and the one which shows the greatest promise as a systematic attempt to devise a technology of instruction, is to be found in the case of programmed learning.

Various reasons for the partial success of the audio-visual aids at present available in schools can be adduced. One of these has to do with inherent limitations in the medium itself. There are, for instance, some things that can only be done superlatively well *only* in a broadcasting studio, but against this it has to be recognized that there are whole realms of meaning which are ruled out because radio is 'blind'. Under what circumstances, and for what purposes, is it true that 'a picture is worth a thousand words'? Just how and why does a diagram give a clearer and more economic explanation than the best of verbal accounts? When is colour essential? And movement? What kinds of experiences are needed in the fostering of the visual intelligence of the future artist, and how do they differ from those required for the future scientist? To these and a host of other questions there are, as yet, no precise answers: and as a consequence those responsible for the manufacture of visual aids are left to carry on their business as best they can with hit-or-miss procedures. In the case of film or television, which combine aural and visual appeal, it may be thought the handicaps are less serious, but here again the producer often finds that he has to resort to makeshifts and improvisations. More often than not, the techniques at his disposal, the taboos and conventions he has to observe are those which have already been perfected by the medium as a form of popular entertainment. In a general way, it is clear that some school subjects lend themselves more readily to visual treatment than others. What is not clear – and the list of desiderata is so extensive that this is the kind of kernel sentence that could be added to indefinitely – is whether such treatment is best provided by television, sound–motion-film, silent film, animated diagrams, or film-strip, whether it is equally desirable and efficacious for 'visualizers' and 'non-visualizers', whether its style varies according to the learner's stage of development, whether its effectiveness depends largely or entirely on judicious timing, and so on. The disembodied voice can communicate the majesty of Miltonic blank verse more directly and more forcefully than its owner can with the book in front of him (as any poetry teacher can prove to his own satisfaction by reading aloud the Messenger's speech in *Samson Agonistes* to a tape recorder and listening to the play-back), but while it is true that there are occasions when sound alone, undistracted by the other senses, excels as a stirrer of the imagination, there are many others in which it finds itself at a hopeless disadvantage.

Despite the non-stop bombardment of visual communication in the modern world, a bombardment which tends more and more to convert young and old alike from readers into viewers, there is much diffusion of effort. Judging by the available evidence, the fact that many schoolchildren spend between two and three hours watching television every night of their lives is not one which need cause teachers to worry over much for the simple reason that the overall effect scholastically – for good or ill – appears to be insignificant. What *should* concern them is the thought that the problems of visual education have barely begun to be investigated. Hitherto there has been no marriage between the techniques of film and television production and the techniques of teaching; and only recently has it been possible to engage film units for the specific purpose of producing materials for use as an integral part of the new schemes of work now being introduced in the schools. This view can be challenged, of course. So far as informal education is concerned, the influence of the mass media has unquestionably been massive. Thanks to broadcasting, the man in the street's musical repertoire is vastly greater than it was fifty years ago. Thanks to television, advertising, and cheap prints his awareness of contemporary styles of painting and architecture is probably keener than it was. Wider dissemination of news and information, it may be thought, has served to raise standards of popular culture just as greater social mobility has served to obscure social-class distinctions.

Fond as we are of saying that one of the chief purposes of education is the 'transmission of culture' we too often forget that these purposes do not comprise the total culture. In any society there are elements of culture – speech, etiquette, moral and emotional attitudes, personality structures, etc – which are acquired incidentally, often unconsciously. Within this supra-system, and constantly influenced by it, is an intra-system which we call formal education. When the pressure from the supra-system increases, as seems to be happening nowadays, a sense of disharmony, at times leading to open conflict, arises. Thus, faced with what it regards as a threat to its academic values from the mass media, the school's first reaction is to close its ranks and maintain a stout resistance to external pressure.

In part this reaction can be explained as being due to sheer conservatism, in part to a sound instinct. So far, in considering the inherent limitations of aural-visual media no mention has been made of the most serious one – the fact that hitherto they have been largely restricted to one-way communication. Not that there is anything insidious in one-way communication as such. The cinema audience, certainly, sees nothing wrong with it, neither does the church congregation at sermon-time, nor the motorist following his road signs, nor the air passenger waiting for his flight to be announced on the public address system. In smaller or larger doses it has its place in the classroom. In short, it is appropriate in situations where there is [a] prior certainty that the 'message' imparted will be understood and [b] no need for continuous interchange of information between sender and receiver. This is not normally the kind of linkage between teacher and pupil, which partakes of the nature of a dialogue. Dialogue ends once the mass media take over. Moreover, their style of display, its content and pacing, are fixed and cannot be altered at the receiving end. While it is true that film, radio, and television each has a unique contribution to make it is also true that they all suffer from an inability to accommodate themselves to the individual learner's needs and problems.

> No matter how carefully tailored they may be to their audience there *is* no way of fitting them to the idiosyncracies of this or that child. . . . Those who are at the receiving end cannot stop the flow of information; when puzzled they cannot ask questions and receive an answer on the spot. If they lose the thread, or misunderstand what the speaker is saying, not matter – the stream of words or pictures, or both, pours over them uninterruptedly. Any difficulties encountered on the way must be set aside until the machine is switched off, and the teacher can try to resolve them in the follow-up after the broadcast or film has ended. This is not to say that children listening to a school broadcast or watching an educational film remain entirely passive, simply to make the point that in radio, television, film (and in books too for that matter), the information flows from one source – producer, broadcaster, film-maker, author – to the learner without the latter being able to influence its course in any way. No amount of excellence in presentation can alter the fact that any possibility of two-way communication occurring has to be ruled out in a mass medium.[2]

Needless to say, this is not necessarily the case in the mass-production of *all* teaching aids. In recent years there has been a growing preference for mechanical devices which enable the teacher to retain immediate control of the classroom situation and which permit pupils to stop and start them at will. In the medium of sound, school broadcasts and commercial recordings still have their place, but the trend nowadays is towards the tape recorder and the language-laboratory. A similar progression is discernible in the visual media: indeed, if we take the series chronologically – blackboard, magic lantern, film-strip, motion film, concept film, overhead projector – it may be thought that the wheel has come full circle. Current developments in the field of closed-circuit television may be taken as representing the first step in the same direction. In each case, the survival value of the mechanical device depends on two factors: first, its efficiency as a significant supplement to the teacher's work, and, second, its flexibility in usage.

As the market for such devices grows, and as customers become more choosy, the laws of supply and demand will presumably operate rather more equably than they do at present. To date, it has to be said, the market for teaching aids has increased at a rate which is out of all proportion to the intrinsic merits of the goods on sale to the schools. In theory, no doubt, the development of the school hardware industry has been spurred by the shortage of teachers: in practice it owes more to commercial enterprise than to any other single factor. The high-pressure salesmanship of gadgets advertising themselves as teaching machines at a time when adequate programmes to feed into them were not available provides only one example of commercial enterprise rushing in where educationists fear to tread. Without going so far as to say that there is too much horse-trading between manufacturers and administrators, the peddling of package deals involving teacher-proof materials needs to be watched very carefully. Instrumentation is one thing, a technology of instruction quite another; and the trouble is that the second takes a good deal longer to perfect than does the first.

Against this, it can be argued that some of the mechanical devices now at the teacher's disposal have outstripped his ability to use them effectively. In the hands of an enterprising teacher a simple tape recorder can be put to a hundred and one different uses so as virtually to transform an otherwise humdrum classroom routine. So, too, can an overhead projector. Why, then, is it uncommon to find such gadgets being put to their fullest possible use? Is it because the enterprising teacher remains a *rara avis*?

The imputation is uncalled for, surely. As a class, teachers have received insufficient training and practice in the use of mechanical devices: for economic reasons, among others, they have had too few opportunities for acquiring the skills involved in handling them to realize what the possibilities are. As more and more devices become available it may be anticipated that teachers will become more adept, but this is unlikely to happen if 'more and more' is to mean a multitude of gadgets each designed according to its own specifications to do this, that, or the other job. In a sense, there are too many aids as it is. Their catalogue is bewildering in its diversity. Too often the convenience obtained at the turn of a switch is purchased dearly in terms of the teacher's time. The equipment comes in bits and pieces, all shapes and sizes, and having procured it the teacher is often at a loss when it comes to trying it out. The more expensive the installation, the greater the need for expertise.

As one critic puts it,

> We would not dream of saying to a medical student, 'Here, this device is a sphygmomenometer. We don't know enough about it to tell you how to use it, or for what purpose it is best suited. Just use your own intuition and it will be of some help doing something.' Nor would we say, 'We can't give you any performance specifications. Just go out there and use your intuition to cure the whole patient.' Yet this is exactly what we do with teachers. We give them very little technology. We don't give them the skills needed to use the world of media to the best advantage. We don't give them precise objectives, procedures, or techniques.[3]

It is a telling thrust, and it cuts both ways. On the other hand, there has been far too little joint-consultation between the makers and the users of audio-visual aids, with the former setting the pace and assuming the role of providing bodies. On the other hand, the teaching profession must share some of the blame for its diffidence and distrust of mechanization in the classroom in any shape or form.

Ultimately, no doubt, it will be recognized that the case for developing a systematic technology of instruction does not rest on expediency – in alleviating the teacher-shortage, for example, or in raising the teacher's status from the amateur to the professional level – still less on novelty for its own sake: on the contrary, it insists that there is no other way of increasing the output and enhancing the quality of the teacher's work. In the meantime, unfortunately, it is not evident, to say the least, how this large claim can be substantiated. With so many aids to choose from, the conscientious teacher who tries his hand at only a few soon finds that his duties become more, not less, exacting – a fact which his not-so-conscientious colleagues, who are content to carry on without them, cannot fail to notice.

To account for this mixed-up state of affairs by saying that most teachers have been slow to come to terms with the new media of communication is not good enough. The truth of the matter is that there is a serious dislocation between the aims and values of formal education (the infra-system) and those of contemporary society at large (the supra-system). The latter is not only forcing the pace, it is also affecting the modes of thought and feeling of people, especially the young, as never before. Those in charge of the new media, therefore, cannot escape the responsibility of coming to terms with the old, failing which the dislocation would become absolute. This, incidentally, explains the 'horseless-carriage syndrome', as it has been called. Invariably, whenever a new invention comes into popular use, its design copies the familiar one which it replaces. Thus, initially, the film is conceived of as the 'film of the book' with the screen copying the décor of the theatrical stage, the television programme becomes a play-back of the film, and Telstar, in turn, becomes a vehicle for the television programme.

Except for the McLuhans of this world, understanding media calls for insights which are all-too uncommon. It takes time – and there is too little time to spare. Cultural change is taking place at a rate which cannot be slowed down and which is already too fast for the school system to cope with comfortably. One of the main reasons is that our whole way of thinking about education has been conditioned by the centuries-old habit of reading continuous prose: we are creatures of print, heirs to a book-dominated culture.

This is becoming less and less true of the rising generation. Not for them the leisurely, rolling sentences of Sir Walter Scott: instead, they are accustomed to the slick, kaleidoscopic mosaic of sight-sound presentation of film and television. Like ducks to water, they take to all the tricks of production – flashbacks, cuts, close-ups, montage shots and the like – tricks which children only thirty years ago would have found utterly incomprehensible. Call it jazzed-up if you like, the stuff of which whizz-kids are made – nevertheless its impact (and the way of life it encourages) is very different from the calm of mind induced in print-oriented learning and thinking.

The extended use of audio-visual aids may be interpreted as an attempt to meet this new learning situation half-way. It implies the admission that conventional methods of teaching are fated to appear tame and ineffectual unless they are suitably enlivened, an admission which is too often made in the spirit of if-you-can't-beat-them-join-them.

A more sober appraisal of the needs of the time is offered by Professor Patrick Meredith:

> The scope and depth of our educational intentions have been widened and enriched by every new communicative medium which an inventive technology has added to our repertoire. When the human voice was the only teaching instrument, all messages had to be conceived in verbal terms. But as man learned to draw, to paint, to write, to print, to make machines and models and instruments, to take photographs, to make them move, to preserve sound on disc and tape, to transmit sound and light over unlimited distances, and now with computers and oscilloscopes to mount flexible and controllable displays of images whose content can be varied at will, our educational intentions are tending to lag behind the power of our media for transmitting them.[4]

More serious still, he thinks, is the growing tendency for our educational thinking to become restricted to *son et lumière* modes, as if the learning process were somehow confined to two sense-channels only. While it may seem merely far-fetched to urge that there is a dangerous neglect of the other senses (which in any case have always played second fiddle in scholastic learning), it is not unreasonable to look for a multi-media technology of instruction. The tools exist. Each has its part to play – television camera, computer, film projector, talking typewriter, light-pencil and the rest. The trouble is that they are so horribly unco-ordinated, rather like the spare parts of an engine which need to be fitted together before they can be made to work properly. When a way of meshing them in an overall communication system is found – and the chances are that this will be sooner rather than later – we shall at last have something worthy of being called a teaching machine.

But before that happens, however, the approach work to a viable technology of instruction will have to be carried a good deal further than it has so far. And in one sector, at least, the progress reports are favourable.

PROGRAMMED LEARNING

In the growing family of educational innovations, programmed learning figures as Thursday's child. This lusty adolescent has far to go, certainly; and it has travelled far and fast during the first twelve years of its existence. In that short time it has alternatively raised and dashed the hopes of its sponsors (among them the learning theorists and the manufacturers of school hardware), while its features have changed so considerably that no one can foretell what it will look like, let alone what will become of it, once it reaches the years of discretion.

To write anything on the subject of programmed learning is to run the risk of being outdated by events. In this field, more so than most, reputations are made and lost with unnerving rapidity. It seems only yesterday that the gospel according to Skinner was being bandied about by his associates and disciples as if it were Holy Writ. Today much of it has come to seem slightly *vieux jeu*. Fresh contenders have changed both the personnel of leadership and its direction; and as the volume and variety of experimental

Infant reading: flash cards for word recognition

Arithmetic: ten-year-olds with Dienes apparatus

Computers at Sevenoaks School. On the table a commercial model. The one at the back was built at the school.

projects and research studies have increased the dogmas of the pioneers have receded with the background.

Kicking off with a fine flourish of self-advertisement in the late fifties and early sixties (– 'learning time cut by half!', 'individual tutoring', 'success guaranteed', 'no instructor needed', 'cheat-proof, package loaded', etc, etc), the teaching machine movement promised to usher in the age of auto-instruction overnight. Ingenuous souls even professed to descry in it a return to the Socratic method. For various reasons, the main one being that the impossible always takes a little longer, the first flush of optimism was short-lived; and a good thing, too, for the indifferent success (or partial failure, depending upon the viewpoint) of the first rudimentary models to be marketed has provided a breathing-space in which programmers can get down to the basic problems of instruction and refine their techniques. By comparison, the problem of instrumentation is of secondary importance. In a way, therefore, the fact that the first so-called teaching machines proved to be a little better than page-turners, with a very limited usefulness, was a blessing in disguise. The programmers were luckier than they knew. Unlike their colleagues in educational tele-vision and film, they did not have a fully perfected machine tech-nology behind them at the start, nor a set of conventions foisted on them from mass media usage: they had to begin from scratch, and with the requirements of formal instruction firmly in mind.

At the moment, then, it is fair to say that programmed learning finds itself in the trough of a wave. For its design experts, it is a case of 'back to the drawing board'. Time is needed, too, for the rank and file of teachers to familiarize themselves with the new materials and equipment that have found their way into the schools, to assess their effectiveness, above all to grasp the principles upon which programming techniques depend. How much longer it will be before machine technology makes possible a new leap forward remains to be seen, though with a computer-based phase of pro-gramming already in sight the need for fast forward-thinking cannot be stressed too strongly. Multi-media systems of communi-cation may not be round the next corner exactly, but in this game,

L

as in life, the only safe assumption is that it is later than we think. In any case, the need for a firmly grounded methodology is paramount.

This being so, it may not be amiss to review the progress of programmed learning to date, and to consider some of the changes it has undergone. In doing so, it will be convenient to distinguish between its past, present, and prospective phases of development

FIRST PHASE: LINEAR AND BRANCHING PROGRAMMES

Amid the conflict of rival persuasions, claims and counter-claims it is easy to forget that all programmers share a common purpose: to convert the craft of teaching (often defined as the art of causing pupils to learn) into a systematic technique. This was Skinner's original intention. Regardless of the criticism levelled against the theory and practice of programming which he expounded that intention remains unchallenged. To achieve at least 90 per cent success with 90 per cent of the population is more than can be bargained for with standard classroom procedures, and to say that programming sets out to achieve nothing less may sound too tall an order. Nevertheless, in industrial training and in the armed forces, where the '90 per cent success' requirement is often vital, the use of programmed materials, with or without machines, has shown that (under certain conditions) it can be done. It is no accident that both the RAF and USAF (which has poured billions of dollars into large-scale projects, besides enlisting the services of some of the best brains in the business) have been actively interested in programming from the start.

So far as teachers are concerned, the reaction has been rather more cautious. This is understandable. After all, the problems encountered in industrial and military training, even in the absence of a competent instructor, are relatively cut-and-dried, nothing like so subtle in their complexity as those involved in the process of *education*. To the extent that programming affords some hope of relieving them from the drudgery of mechanical tasks, some teachers are prepared to welcome it with open arms. A few are enthusiastic enough to engage in that most astringent of all academic exercises – writing and testing their own programmes. The numbers actually using programmed materials continue to grow, but remain disappointingly small. (A survey carried out by the Programmed Instruction Centre in Middlesex during the 1963–1964 academic year estimated that only 2 per cent of the primary schools and $3\frac{1}{2}$ per cent of the secondary schools in the county were using programmes.* These figures are comparable with the 2–5 per cent estimate arrived at by a Center for Programmed Instruction nation-wide survey in the USA during the year 1961–1962.†) The vast majority, it seems, have 'heard about it' and are mildly intrigued, waiting on the side-lines. Throughout the country, local and regional groups have sprung up more or less spontaneously, and the numbers attending short, intensive courses for programme writers organized by educational and other bodies continue to increase.

The salient features of the technique will presumably be familiar to most readers and can, in any case, be briefly enumerated:

1] The learning objectives are clearly specified in terms of the learner's eventual performance
2] The necessary instructions and information are presented in a carefully ordered sequence
3] This pre-determined sequence is arrived at empirically
4] Throughout, the learner is required to be an active participant – normally, at each step he has to respond to the instruction before carrying on to the next step
5] Normally, the learner proceeds at his own individual rate
6] Normally, he receives immediate confirmation of the correctness or incorrectness of his response.

Salient features, unfortunately, do not add up to a set of first principles. Although devout Skinnerians continue to deny it,

* But note that *29* per cent of further education establishments in the Middlesex survey said that they were using programmed materials.

† According to the Texas State Agency 27 per cent of the schools were using or planning to use programmed instruction in 1965–66.

1. At each step in a linear programme you have to answer a question. Normally, the assumption is that there can be only —— correct answer.

2. Because of this, none of the questions can be left open-ended. Invariably, they have to be framed so as to leave no doubt about the essential correctness of the ——.

3. In so far as the aim is simply to impart factual information this limitation raises no difficulty for the programme-writer. In factual subjects there is only —— possible —— to most questions.

4. Facts are facts, we often say, implying that there is no point in arguing about them. In other words, facts are not really open to q——.

5. Factual information is sometimes referred to as POSITIVE KNOW-LEDGE, i.e. knowledge which can be tested and verified, the certainty of which can be proved. In the sense that people do not argue about it, —— knowledge is not open to question.

6. Thus, most of the knowledge acquired in scientific subjects is said to be ——.

7. On the other hand, Religion, Philosophy, and the Arts generally embrace forms of knowledge which are much more open to question and which therefore cannot be described as ——.

8. To the extent that there is a 'Great Divide' between the Arts and the Sciences, then, it looks as though a linear programme will be more effective in the —— than in the ——.

9. In the Arts the answers to many important questions will depend upon some kind of VALUE JUDGMENT. Different individuals will tend to give different answers according to their personal taste or ——.

[7]

---

1. one	6. positive
2. answer	7. positive
3. one answer	8. Sciences / Arts
4. question	9. opinion (preference, choice)
5. positive	

FIG 7   A typical page from a linear programme
(with answers added)

more than one of the points in the above list is now open to serious question. It is by no means certain, for instance, that it is *always* a good thing to allow the pupil to work at the rate which he feels suits him best. It is even less certain that programmed learning must inevitably interpret itself as self-instruction. The need for some form of continuous active response is not denied, but to insist on it invariably at every step seems doctrinaire; and to do so without ensuring that the nature and quality of the response are appropriate to the learning situation – as happens all-too frequently in programmed texts which call for nothing more than the filling in of missing words – is futile. As for immediate confirmation – 'knowledge of results' as it is called – we need to know a great deal more about the conditions in which it is advantageous: all that can be said at the moment is that under certain circumstances it is evidently not so indispensable as we have been led to suppose.

The original model adopted in linear programmes was, of course, derived from the psychology of operant conditioning. It assumes that changes in behaviour (which are regarded as being synonymous with learning) can best be brought about by arranging 'schedules of reinforcement', i.e. rewarding the desired behaviour at appropriate points, as in animal-training. To this end, the 'terminal behaviour' is first defined and the subject-matter or skill which has to be learned is broken down into a series of minute steps. Each step consists of [a] an item of information (which may be given directly or indirectly in the form of prompts), [b] a question (often implied) to test the learner's understanding, by eliciting [c] the appropriate response. Usually the information leads infallibly to the correct answer. Apart from taking pains to ensure that, so far as possible they do not occur, linear programming makes no provision for the correction of errors.

Leaving aside the many objections which can be raised against Skinner's learning theory (not least its profound misunderstanding of the part played by language in human learning), hard-won experience of the methods used in linear programmes suggests the following conclusions:

1] Normally, a linear programme is a fixed sequence, i.e. all pupils receive the same information and follow the same set of instructions. (It is true that skip sequences can be introduced, but this is at best a clumsy device and one which is not frequently resorted to in published programmes.)

2] Post-test scores show a distribution which is usually more homogeneous than the distribution of marks in an examination based on conventional methods of teaching. Average and below-average pupils tend to do as well as, and sometimes better than, the bright ones. The long 'tail' of failures or near-failure is reduced, if it does not disappear altogether.

3] At the same time, the original contention that the same programme serves equally well for the bright and the dull pupils has been shown to be false. The evidence indicates fairly conclusively that, to be fully effective, a linear programme needs to be specially designed and prepared for a particular age and ability group.

4] In general, it is safe to say that a linear programme loses little or nothing in being presented in the form of a text. Housing it in a machine slows down the rate of progress, and, in practice, has nothing to recommend it, except possibly in the case of very young pupils. (Sidney Pressey, G.O.M. of the movement rightly derides the Skinner box – 'about as hampering as a scanning device which required one to look at a picture only 1 square inch at a time'.)[5] As regards the danger of cheating, the research evidence is, to say the least of it, equivocal.

5] Linear programmes can be tolerably effective at all age and ability levels. This is not to say that they always *are*, simply that experience shows that learners at all stages from pre-school pupils to post-graduate students find the small-step approach acceptable – and one which they often prefer to lessons or lectures.

6] In the present state of the art, linear programmes are most successful when taken in small doses. They are least effective, and may be worse than useless, in the absence of sympathetic monitoring and assistance on the part of the teacher. For the latter to withdraw his support and expect the programme to do the job for him by itself is quite inexcusable.

7] For his part, the linear programme-writer does well to recognize that he is ill-advised to attempt to tackle entire courses. As a teaching instrument (at any rate so long as it remains in the form of a paper text) his device may come in handy for cracking nuts, but not for moving mountains!

8] By far the great majority of programmes can be classified as belonging to the linear type. This is true of those which are produced commercially as well as those written by private individuals. Ironically, although the pundits never tire of apologizing for the crudity of the technique and of dissociating themselves from its prime mover, the fact remains that nearly everyone ends up writing linear programmes. To some extent, this widespread popularity may be due to a beggars-cannot-be-choosers philosophy: after all, frame-writing can be done by anyone who has a pencil and jotter. Again, the resulting text is a straightforward affair – which is more than can be said for even the least complicated lay-out of a scrambled book.

9] Finally, it has to be noted that most linear programmes deal with mathematical, scientific or technical subjects. How far this repertoire can be explained in terms of supply and demand and how far to limitations in the technique itself remains arguable. In theory, the assumption that any subject can be programmed provided that it can be taught is almost certainly valid, but even so it does not follow that all subjects lend themselves equally well, if at all, to small-step treatment. It is not obvious, for example, how history can profitably be dealt with in this way.

It is, of course, tempting to say that teachers of the humanities have been less willing and less thoroughgoing than their colleagues

in science in exploring the possibilities. Alternatively, their reluctance to do so may well have arisen from a sound judgement.
Without necessarily appealing to the *Geisteswissenschaften-Natur-
wissenschaften* dualism, teachers of English, history, music,
or RI are surely within their rights in saying that the cognitive
processes with which they are concerned call for insight and
intuition – 'exercises for the left hand' in Bruner's parlance – and
that these too often elude the mechanical lockstep of a fixed
sequence.

Be this as it may, it has to be conceded that most of the early
applications of the linear technique to literary and aesthetic topics
have turned out to be singularly unimaginative and tasteless. For
that matter, strict adherence to 'Skinnerian principles' has a lot
to answer for: regardless of the topic, the fault of most small-step
programmes is that they are horribly *over-programmed*.

Still, with all its faults, linear programming works, at any rate
after a fashion. Maybe it leaves something to be desired in equating
the problem of instruction with the systematic and controlled
presentation of *information*; but at least in concentrating on this
side of the problem it has performed a useful service.

Intrinsic (or branching) programming seeks to redress the
balance. In the words of its leading practitioner, 'The student's
choice of an answer to a multiple-choice question can be used
automatically to direct him to new material. . . . In intrinsic
programming the question serves primarily a diagnostic purpose,
and the basis of the technique is the fact that the diagnosis so made
can be promptly utilized to furnish specific remedial material to
the student.' In his view, a low error-rate cannot be taken as the
sole guarantee, still less the sole criterion, of successful learning.
The most carefully prepared fixed sequence cannot hope to cater
for individual differences; and it is mere sophistry to pretend that
it does so by reducing its explanations to the level of the meanest
intellect.

'Basically, it comes down to the problem posed by human
variability,' Crowder maintains. 'The more carefully we fit the
microstructure of instructional materials to a single individual, the

less good must be the fit for a second individual. We can attain the illusion of fitting everyone if we judge only by the student's success in giving the correct responses, since in general a good student can do what a dull student can, but surely this is naïve.'[6]

The force of the objection is not to be denied. It hinges on the fact that the questions asked in a linear programme must always be of the true-false variety, admitting of only one possible answer. Now, clearly, there are many questions which admit of alternative answers. Suppose, for instance, that there are two equally acceptable choices. In a three-step sequence this yields 2^3 possibilities.

STEP 1   STEP 2   STEP 3

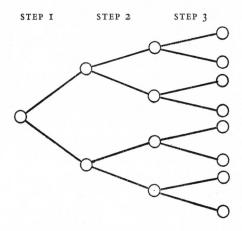

Contrast this with the rigidy of a linear sequence, where everyone has no option but to follow the same route.

STEP 1   STEP 2   STEP 3

Crowder's main reason for preferring multiple-choice questions, therefore, is that the student's response not only deserves to be treated on its merits but also affords vital information about how his mind is working. Without this information, the instructor is left in the dark. The response may be the one that is desired, or it may be a near miss, or hopelessly wide of the mark: no matter, whatever it is, the response is revealing. If it is correct, well and good, the student can proceed to the next step as in a linear programme. If it is a near miss, he may be guided to the correct answer at a second attempt. Failing this, he may need to be given additional advice and information and try a third or fourth time. If he still does not succeed, he can be shunted back on to a more elementary sequence.

This, more or less, is the strategy adopted in a branching programme:

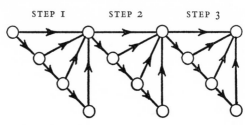

To the extent that everyone arrives at the same destination, while following different routes, this is a rather more flexible arrangement. Indeed, seeing that so many sound pedagogical arguments seem to be on their side, it may be wondered why the Crowderians have not carried the day.

A moment's reflection prompts the explanation. Briefly, a branching strategy *is* more flexible than the one allowed for in a fixed sequence, *but not flexible enough*. The provision of three or four alternative choices (the most that can be bargained for in a scrambled book) caters for individual differences only to a very limited extent. In mathematical, scientific, and technical fields, where the subject-matter has its own internal logical structure, it is possible to anticipate most or all the errors which the learner is likely to make. This being so, the main-line sequence can be pre-determined without much difficulty, as happens in a linear programme. In other fields, however, the internal structure is less self-evident, with the result that any sequence tends to be much more a function of the learner's responses.

The difference between the two types of material is a fundamental one and, we feel, is related to the orderliness of the subject material.

Orderliness is probably best measured by the number of possible correct responses. For example, in stenotype a stimulus word may be associated with only one correct response – a specific simultaneous depression of a particular set of keys. In a philosophy course, however, one might be faced with the question, 'What is love?' The number of combinations of different words that can be used to answer this question (to somebody's satisfaction) is enormous; therefore this question would be considered poorly organized. It is our feeling that the earliest success with computerized teaching machines will be with well-ordered material.[7]

What it amounts to is that the branching technique, while representing a distinct advance, does not go far enough to justify the extra trouble involved in its exercise. More often than not, all that happens in a typical Tutor Text (scrambled book) is that the reader is told to think again before being referred back to the original question. The result sequence follows a kind of herring-bone pattern.

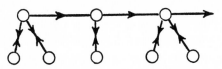

When installed in a machine of the Auto Tutor or Grundytutor type, genuinely remedial sub-sequences become rather more manageable, but even here the built-in strategy has to be a very simple one. One obvious limitation of such machines is their inability to monitor the learner's performance while it is still in progress: the various responses are registered on a counting device, but this information cannot be used in directing the course of events, only to chart it when it is finished. Another criticism, and one which the Skinnerians press with vigour, concerns the nature of push-button responses: *selecting* an answer from a given set of alternatives is not the same as *constructing* one.

It is easy to conclude that the holy war between the Skinnerians and the Crowderians has hindered rather than advanced the cause of programmed learning, and that the rival champions are to blame for defending their positions in so entrenched, not to say stiff-necked, a manner. Easy enough to play the peacemaker by saying that each method has its place and that the two can be combined. So they can in practice. To be sure, there is nothing to prevent a linear programmer inserting a branching sequence as and when it suits his purpose, and vice versa.

But to foster a bastard breed is no way to develop a technology of any sort. Historically and theoretically, the two methods have little in common: they arise from diametrically opposed assumptions about the learning process which admit of no compromise. In the event, the linear approach has gained the more widespread acceptance despite the fact that several of its alleged 'first principles' – the need for small steps, the need for a low error-rate, the need for rigorous control over the learner's behaviour, the need for overt responses, and the identification of 'knowledge of results' with 'reinforcement' – are not above reproach.* A practice which works despite the theory on which it rests may be justified on pragmatic grounds, but only temporarily. Evidently, a more soundly established theory is needed. On balance, then, there must be sympathy for Crowder's position in maintaining that the two techniques have different purposes in mind and are, to that extent, irreconcilable.

> The basic difference, which so often goes unrecognised, between lineal and intrinsic programming is the fact that each is concerned with a different part of the educational process. The linear programs are directed to improving the microstructure of the process, i.e. they seek methods whereby the student can be made infallibly to learn at each step. The intrinsic programmers are not convinced that the microstructure can be sufficiently improved that the success of each step can be assumed, at least at a tolerable cost in redundancy, and so

* 'In general we have found no evidence to support the widely held belief that programs must consist of very easy frames and must require overt written responses. Under the experimental conditions reported, we find learning level to be a function of an interaction between item difficulty and mode of response.'

(J. J. Briggs et al, 'Experimental Results regarding form of response, size of step, and individual differences in automated programs', pp. 96–97, *Programmed Learning and Computer-based Instruction*, Wiley, 1962.)

are interested in the possibilities of manipulating the macrostructure of the process, by continually testing the student and utilizing the test result to vary the materials presented to the student. Nowhere can the essential difference in the two techniques be seen so clearly as when we ask the programmer's purpose in eliciting a response from the student. The linear programmer elicits the response because he believes that the making of the response is an essential part of the learning process. Once a response has been elicited, it has served its purpose (in a linear program) and no further use is made of it. In an intrinsic program, the programmer elicits the response in order to see if the student has learned, because this information will be used to determine whether the next point is to be presented, or whether additional information on the previous point is required. . . . The basic difference is not in the form of the student's response but rather in the purpose served by requiring him to make a response at all.[8]

SECOND PHASE: LEARNING OBJECTIVES AND LEARNING SETS

While it would be misleading to pretend that the reaction of second generation programmers has been to say, 'A plague on both your houses', there has undoubtedly been a shift of emphasis. The nature of the shift is akin to that which took place earlier in the field of educational theory and announced itself as the child-centred doctrine. *Absit omen!* Dissatisfied with the theoretical models of the old school, and the lockstep practice which they imposed, the new school has addressed itself to the problems of instruction from new angles. The stress on systematic, frame-by-frame presentation of *information* has to some extent given way to concepts which envisage the learning process more in terms of guided *inquiry*.

The change of direction is nicely illustrated in a minuscule publication which appeared in 1961 under the title of 'Preparing Objectives for Programmed Instruction'. As pithy a piece of pedagogy as ever was written, its 50-odd pages should be made prescribed reading for all practising teachers and students in training, for what it has to say concerns them just as much as it does would-be programmers.

In Mager's judgement it is not enough for the programmer to define the 'terminal behaviour' and leave it at that, for the same reason that it is not enough for the teacher to state his educational aim and then sit back and hope for the best. In so far as it is concerned with ends rather than means, educational theory must, of course, have something to say about ultimate aims. The trouble is that these tend to be couched in such amorphous terms – 'the nurture of personal growth', say, or 'intelligent citizenship' – that they degenerate too easily into loose talk. As a class, educationists have a weakness for discussing aims without doing much or anything about them. Mager's little book disclaims any intention of dealing with the ethical question of what constitutes a good, or even a desirable, goal. What it sets out to do is to show how such goals can be stated in terms calculated to be meaningful and useful to instructor and student alike, and in this it succeeds admirably.

The distinction drawn between an 'aim' and an 'objective' involves far more than a verbal quibble. An *aim* looks good on paper, but normally it flatters to deceive. Too often it tends to be implicit rather than explicit, something which the teacher keeps to himself. By contrast, the whole point of an *objective* is that it tells the learner what he is expected to do, what the minimum level of acceptance for his eventual performance is to be, and under what conditions it will be achieved. To be useful, any statement of objective must specify observable (preferably measurable) changes in the learner's behaviour at the end of the course.

'A meaningful stated objective, then, is one that succeeds in communicating your intent; the best statement is one that excludes the greatest number of possible alternatives to your goal.'[9]

Accordingly, in writing down an objective it is advisable to avoid using ambiguous words ('understand', 'know', 'appreciate', etc) which are open to slippery interpretations and to prefer those ('identify', 'differentiate', etc) which are more amenable to verification. Thus, instead of saying that the aim of a physics lesson is, 'To develop an understanding of the theory of combustion', the list of objectives might read as follows:

'When you have worked through this programme you will be able to,

1] Describe one way in which a scientist might answer the question, "What is necessary for combustion?"

2] Show hot water can be made to boil in a paper dish without burning the paper,

3] State several hypotheses (guesses) as to why the paper does not burn

4] Carry out experiments to find out which hypothesis is correct

5] Say how a scientist might explain the results of the experiments which you have carried out, and

6] Say how the findings of your experiments might be put to practical use.'

In each case, the *objective* is so specific as to be readily testable. This is more than can be said for the larger *aim*, which remains indefinite.

For the instructor, then, a statement of objectives has two functions:

a] it helps to clarify his intentions;

b] it makes it easier for him to gauge the extent to which his intentions have been fulfilled.

For the student, likewise, a statement of objectives has two functions:

a] it provides him with a framework of expectation, i.e. it tells him what the instructor wants him to do, so that he is not left guessing;

b] it helps him to evaluate his progress.

In short, an objective is prescriptive, not merely descriptive of the content of the course to be followed. It states an intended outcome and does so in terms of the learner's actual performance. If it is to succeed in communicating the instructor's intentions as to what the learner will be able to do at the end of the course (and thereafter) it must:

'[a] Identify and name the overall behaviour act.

[b] Define the important conditions under which the behavior is to occur (givens and/or restrictions and limitations).

[c] Define the criterion of acceptable performance.'[10]

To those who protest that the subjects they teach are too full of imponderables to be reduced to such rule-of-thumb treatment Mager has this to say: 'Well ... all right ... but if you are teaching skills which cannot be evaluated you are in the awkward position of being unable to demonstrate that you are teaching anything at all. While it is true in general that the more important an objective is the more difficult it is to state, we can go a long way toward stating objectives a good deal better than has been done until now.'[11]

The full significance of Mager's insistence on the need for precisely stated objectives ('the more statements you have, the better the chance you have of making clear your intent', he says) is to be seen in his final advice: 'If you give each learner a copy of your objectives you may not have to do much else'.[12] Instead of having the programmer determine the order of presentation frame by frame, why not let the learner decide the order for himself? What seems a necessary or logical order to the instructor may not appear so to the student. For example, Mager notes that whereas most electronics courses take electron theory or magnetism as the 'obvious' starting-point, his own students almost invariably began by asking about the workings of the vacuum tube. By first giving them a set of objectives for the course and then leaving them to seek information and guidance from the instructor *only* as and when they feel the need for it, he suggests learning becomes more efficient than it does under more rigidly controlled conditions.

On the face of things, then, the wheel has come full circle from Skinner to Mager. So far as adults are concerned, the latter's view may be summed up by saying that half the battle has been won once they have been given the objectives. How far, if at all,

The language-laboratory at Tonbridge School

The University of Glasgow Television Service's outside broadcast unit. Equipped with four television cameras and a miniature control room, it relays lectures and records lectures and demonstrations on videotape for later use by the University and other establishments. (Photo courtesy of Marconi.)

An IBM 1440 computer. (Photo: courtesy of IBM.)

it is safe to rely on this policy of giving them the tools and leaving them to get on with the job of learning in the case of the mass of schoolchildren remains open to question. To the extent that it is willing to transfer the onus, where possible and so far as possible, from the instructor to the learner such a policy is at least in keeping with the heuristic methods recommended by the curricular re-formers. At the heart of it is the conviction that, in the last analysis, the learner must be treated as a responsible agent and that the approach he brings to the learning situation (including his attitudes, hopes and fears as well as his cognitive skills) is as important a consideration as any. Here again, the new-style programmer is in sympathy with those educationists who see 'predispositions' as the key to any theory of instruction.

> We said, 'Right. What the student can do at the end of the course is important, but what we are mainly concerned with is what he will be able to do at some time in the future.' This conclusion was reached after careful inspection of educational objectives prepared by nationally recognized educators. No matter how many we looked at we found they all had one thing in common: they all intend for the student to be able to do something at some point in time *after* the instruction has ended, at some point after the influence of the instructor is terminated.
>
> 'Well,' we said, 'suppose we really wanted to take these objectives seriously. Suppose we really wanted to do everything we can to reach these objectives. What could we do?'
>
> This question led us to a rather startling conclusion. That conclusion was that no matter what the nature of the instruction, no matter what the subject matter, no matter what the age level of the student, there is a universal objective appropriate to all instruction; that *at the very least* it should be the intent of the instructor to send the student away from the instruction with an attitude toward the subject matter at *least* as favorable as that with which he arrived.
>
> Why? Because if we are to maximize the probability that a student will use in the future what he has learned, we must at least see that he is *willing* to use his knowledge, we must see to it that he does not run in the opposite direction whenever he is faced with the subject we have taught him; in other words, we must act to see to it we don't

M

teach the student to hate the very subject we are teaching him about. If education is for the future, we teachers must not be the agents through which the student becomes less inclined to come into contact with the very subject we have worked so hard to teach him. Indeed, we must send him away anxious not only to use what he has learned but anxious to learn more about it as time goes on.

'But, really,' we were told, '*every* teacher wants to send his students away more favorably disposed toward his subject than when the student arrived.' And this was the most astonishing point of all. For if this is true, then for the most part it is a hollow wish, it is talk not followed by action, it is little more than another example of good intention. Because, you see, to act to achieve this goal requires that the objective be specified in a way that would allow one to recognize success, some sort of measuring instrument would have to be prepared and administered to ascertain whether attitudes have been improved or degraded by the teacher, course procedures would have to be analyzed for techniques that tend to adversely influence attitude (approach tendency), and the course would have to be constantly monitored for its affective effect on the student. How many are demonstrating that much interest in reaching their instructional objectives?

'There can't be many,' we were told by one ex-student. 'After all,' he said, 'not all of us millions dropped out because we were pregnant.'[13]

According to this thesis, motivation increases as a function of the degree of control, or apparent control, which the learner is allowed to exercise over the learning experience. Given clearly stated objectives, the mature student at any rate is the best person to decide how to reach them by dovetailing what he needs to know with what he already knows. This is essentially different from protecting him from aversive behaviour by putting him through a predetermined sequence of small steps, as happens in a linear programme.

Along with the attempt to develop techniques which permit the learner to find the appropriate sequence for himself goes another – the attempt to systematize methods of detecting the relevant background level ('entry behaviour') of the learner. The pre-test provided for by most programmers is better than nothing, if only as indication of what is not already known, but as a diagnosis it is patently inadequate and quite incapable of disclosing the appropriate starting-point to each individual.

The wide applications of programmed learning in industrial and military training help to explain why task analysis has been so influential in focusing attention on the critical problem of 'entry behaviour'. Task analysis begins by examining what the worker does, how, when and why he does it, and ends by breaking down the skills involved in the operation into its components. These are arranged hierarchically – the bits and pieces which form the operation as a whole – so that their interlocking relationships can be seen. Unless the instructor knows what these components are, the order and the ways in which they are acquired, he must rely on mother wit when it comes to training the novice. On the basis of task analysis he is helped in two ways: [a] the objectives are more closely defined (i.e. the operations which the trainee must be able to perform successfully at the end of the course), and [b] the prerequisite threshold knowledge is more clearly delineated (i.e. the knowledge and skills which can be taken for granted on admission to the course).

Thus, according to Gagné, any theory of productive learning must deal with the interaction of two independent variables, the first of which he calls *instructions*, the other *subordinate capabilities* or *learning sets*.

Instructions are not to be confused with the giving of factual information: they are, rather, directions which lead the learner to find the relevant information for himself. Instructions serve a number of purposes. First, they enable the learner to identify the objectives set for him: in other words, they 'define the goal'. Second, they help to establish high recallability. Third, they serve as signposts for thinking, albeit in ways which remain obscure.

At a minimum, this function of instructions may be provided by a statement like, 'Now put these ideas together to solve this problem'; possibly this amounts to an attempt to establish a *set*. Beyond this, thinking may be guided by suggestions which progressively limit the

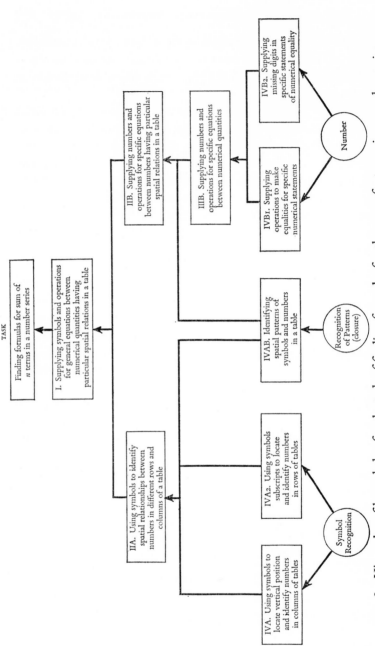

FIG 8 Hierarchy of knowledge for the task of finding formulas for the sum of n terms in a number series

From a diagram published by R. M. Gagné in Educational Technology, ed. De Cecco, Holt, Rinehart and Winston, 1964.

range of hypotheses entertained by the learner, in such a way as to decrease the number of incorrect solutions he considers. . . . In common-sense terms, the purpose of these instructions is to suggest to the learner 'how to approach the solution of a new task' without, however, 'telling him the answer'.[14]

Subordinate capabilities, or *learning sets*, are the very stuff of individual differences. They can only be identified by asking, 'What must the learner be able to do beforehand in tackling each of the various component parts of the task hierarchy?' Accordingly, the analysis begins with the end-product, the task itself. It enumerates the capabilities (concepts, skills, etc) which the learner needs to possess in advance in order to perform it, *given only instructions*. In this way, the new or additional information essential for the final performance, can be defined.

Figure 8 illustrates the procedure. A mathematical task, 'deriving formulas for the sum of *n* terms in a number series', is broken down into nine component *learning sets*. Within limits, the order in which they occur, and the patterns of relationship between them may vary from one individual to another; but failure to master any single one will prevent the successful completion of the final task.

Learning, then, is a matter of transfer of training from a group of *subordinate capabilities* to a new activity which incorporates them at a higher level. This higher level of mental activity is qualitatively different from the ones which precede it and make it possible; and its secret inheres in the combination of old learning sets to form new ones, not simply in being 'more difficult'.

This being so, the programmer's first duty in theory (and the teacher's) is to find the lowest *subordinate capability* for each individual and begin at that point. In practice, needless to say, this amounts to a formidable undertaking.

Which brings the progress report up to date, more or less. That there is a vast amount of unfinished business and a host of problems awaiting solution before anything like an educational technology is arrived at goes without saying. At the same time, it is not premature to affirm that there are visible advances. Whereas the first phase of programming was content to fix the terminal behaviour and concentrate on carefully sequenced presentation of subject-matter, the second has been characterized by its determined attack on the problems of learning-objectives, the structure and approach-work of the learning process.

What does it all add up to? And where do we go from here? In an essay entitled, 'Components of the Instructional Process', Glaser argues that in programmed learning we have the makings of a self-contained system of communication which cannot fail to perfect itself in time. The various parts of the system, which are inter-dependent may be outlined diagrammatically.

	Research and Development Logistics		
Instructional Goals	Entering Behaviour	Instructional Procedures	Performance Assessment
'fixing the terminal behaviour' 'statement of learning objectives', etc.	pre-test diagnostic tests, subordinate capabilities, etc.	linear, branding, computer-based, student-controlled sequences, etc.	post-test, evaluative studies, long-term transfer of training, etc

As he explains,

The main input into the system, upon which it is designed to operate, consists of the entering behavior of the student. This consists of the initial repertoire, aptitude, and prior educational background with which the instructional process begins. The next phase constitutes the actual instructional procedures and experiences which are employed to guide and modify behavior. The final phase in an instructional situation is some sort of 'quality control', that is, assessment of the extent to which the end-of-course behavior has been achieved by the student in the light of the kind of performance required by the specified instructional goals. These phases are the main flow of the instructional system, but it has many feedback loops and subsidiary inputs. The information obtained in each phase supplies data which are useful for monitoring and correcting the output of the preceding phase: for example, measurement of the kind of performance achieved can provide information for re-design of instructional procedures, and information on instructional procedures can interact with the characteristics of the entering behavior. Feeding in to all phases are the results of research and development.[15]

This sounds fine, almost as though future developments could be plotted on a flow-chart. But, then, the language of systems theory suits those who are fond of whistling in the dark and would be more convincing if it were less inflated. On closer inspection, some of the words it uses, like some of the rectangles in the diagrams it draws, turn out to be pretty empty affairs. To say that programmed learning has its 'instructional goals', its inputs of 'entering behaviour', its 'instructional procedures' and the rest – and that these are linked together by 'feedback loops' and what-not – so as to form a going concern tells us nothing that is not equally true of any educational system, any school, or for that matter any teacher.

Against this, there is comfort in the thought that from start to finish testing-as-you-go is the very essence of programming. Strange, therefore, that research studies rarely yield conclusive results. One reason why the verdict 'No significant differences' keeps on recurring with monotonous regularity is that many of these studies have been of the comparative type – linear versus branching programmes, computer-assisted instruction versus scrambled book, programmes versus 'flesh and blood' teachers, overt versus covert responses, teaching machines versus programmed texts, and so on.* Until we know precisely what we are comparing, it seems that no amount of statistical expertise can prevent the findings from such studies being contaminated by a host of extraneous factors: there are too many variables and unknowns to permit of generalizable results. While not necessarily agreeing that, 'Once we knew enough about the population of

* Cf. Paschal N. Strong 'Research Accomplishments and Needs in Programmed Instruction', *Trends in Programmed Instruction*, ed. Ofiesh and Meierhenry, pp. 224–230.

variations that we call auto-instructional programming we may see why a comparative study could not possibly lead to results that would aid in making a useful decision,'[16] it remains true that the criteria for a soundly based technology of instruction have yet to be established. In a sense, this is not only inevitable but all to the good, for it means deferring hard-and-fast judgements until greater experience has been gained and subtler techniques of programming and testing have been worked out.

In the meantime there are grounds for quiet optimism. Invariably, pupils learn *something* from programmes. Possibly the most consistent finding is that they learn at least equally well by this as by other methods of instruction, sometimes better. This, moreover, with imperfect programmes. Since programming has the unique capability of checking the conditions under which learning takes place, it is possible to predict continuous improvement in the efficiency of the technique.

THIRD PHASE: MULTI-MEDIA COMMUNICATION SYSTEMS

The next stage is likely to see instrumentation coming into its own and in a big way. After what looked suspiciously like a false start in the late fifties and early sixties, much more sophisticated teaching machines are now ready to be put through their paces. Anyone who has worked with one of the older models and then transferred to a computer-assisted installation, say the IBM 1440, will immediately sense the enormous advance: it is the difference between riding uphill on a bicycle and being hurtled aloft in a jet aircraft.

Essentially, the equipment used in a typical computer-assisted instruction system consists of [1] a series of storage units, [2] a data-processing or computing unit, [3] a transmission control unit, [4] a temporary storage unit, and [5] individual student terminals, printer keyboards. According to the manufacturers, CAI (computer-assisted instruction) is 'presented, not as a complete solution to any one problem, but as an experimental tool in discovering new dimensions in education'.

From the instructor's point of view, the advantages are immense, the possibilities seemingly limitless. The coursewriter language (i.e. the operation codes and control words for conveying sets of instructions to the computer) is easily learned and does not commit him to any particular method. If he does not happen to be a programmer, he can follow the methods he would normally use in

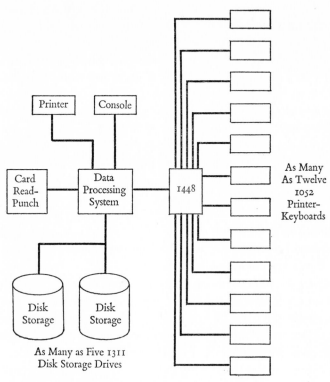

FIG 9 Typical 1440–1448 computer-assisted instruction system configuration

the classroom. Not only can he write his course while the students are actually taking it, but at any point, simply by inserting the control words 'go to', he can signal the computer that he wishes to become a student himself and see how the course is going. Having done so, he can return to his status as instructor simply by typing in the control word 'author'. He can then go back and revise or erase passages which seem to him to be faulty. He can hover around, watching students at work to see how they are progressing or he can study the print-outs and statistical analyses of the students' work which the computer provides during his absence. In this way he is given accurate reports of the results of his course and is free to improve it *while it is still in progress*. Flexibility is built into the system, and much of the hard grind of programme-writing is removed. Information, instructions, assignments, and tests can be typed straight into the printer keyboard and continuously revised, if necessary while the students are at work. The computerized programme can accommodate a vastly wider range of contingencies than can be bargained for in any of the branching techniques developed so far. Whereas the latter can only provide for three or four alternative responses, a computer-assisted programme can cope with almost any number. It can distinguish between fine shades of meaning in the students' responses (to say nothing of those which are unrecognizable) – 'Yes', 'Certainly', 'Of course', 'Probably', 'I think so', 'Possibly', 'Not sure', 'Don't know', or 'I don't understand the question' – and instantly adjust the next item for display to suit the individual's needs.

Again, the storage capacity is immense. As many as five different courses (each of which may include up to two million items) per disk pack can be operated simultaneously. Not only do these house the course material itself, they also monitor and record individual and class performances, besides acting as book-keepers and registrars. The data-processing unit acts as an intermediary between the students and the course material, checking each individual's responses with the various answers listed by the instructor and then following the appropriate instructions. Each student signs on and off as and when he pleases. When several are at work, the traffic of messages is directed by the transmission control unit; and because the interchange is handled almost instantaneously, each student feels that the system is operating for his own special benefit.

The chief paradigm of programmed learning has always been

that of a dialogue between a single tutor and a single student; and with the more flexible give-and-take which becomes possible in computer-assisted instruction co-operation between man and machine really partakes of the character of an exchange of conversation. The student's performance is continuously monitored, so that pacing and level of difficulty can be varied from individual to individual and from one part of the course to another. The fact that he has to type his responses on to a keyboard ensures that he is actively engaged. Synchronized colour-slide, film projectors, and tape recordings can bring sight and sound to bear on the learning process as and when they are needed. In more elaborate installations which incorporate the cathode-ray tube and the 'light pencil' his responses can become pictorial and diagrammatic, not purely verbal or mathematical as they have been hitherto.

Before enthusiasm runs away with common sense, however, it is well to remind ourselves of some of the things that computer-assisted instruction cannot do and will presumably never be able to do. Full automation, when it comes, will not relieve the man behind the machine from the need for hard work and hard thinking, still less of the need for imagination. At the moment, for example, it takes something like 80–100 hours of an author's time to prepare the tapes needed for 1 hour of computer-assisted instruction; and even then, if he is worth his salt, he needs to be on hand, watching each student's performance or going over the print-outs after the student has signed off, to see just where the strategies he has adopted can be improved.

> An automated device cannot take an answer and explore its possibilities in whatever kind of situation can be imagined. Its answers must be available when the pupil begins his tutorship. The best that an automated device could do with 'What is piety?' is to furnish variant answers. How could it frame a direct response to whatever definition, or lack of it, the learner happened to propose? Perhaps responding to a wide open choice given to the learner is within the limits of our most complex computers, but one suspects that responding like Socrates is not.[17]

But perhaps it is high time we stopped talking about the inability of the machine to match the wisdom of Socratic teaching (a rare commodity under the best of circumstances, and one which has never had much of a place in the average classroom anyway) and recognize its manifold abilities, which are nothing short of staggering. Time, too, to recognize that the economic argument against putting these abilities to practical use is certain to be short-timed. Granted, the capital outlay for the central installation will continue to be heavy in the foreseeable future, but separate terminals can be dispersed over a wide area (ultimately, no doubt, in the student's home) and as the number increases rentals will be reduced. Even with as few as half a dozen terminals, the estimated cost per student-hour for computer-assisted instruction at the University of Texas is only $2\frac{1}{2}$ dollars, which compares favourably with the cost of lecturing. Instead of going ahead with expensive closed-circuit television networks, local education authorities might be well advised to think twice: in the long run the chances are that for normal school purposes a computer-based installation will prove to be much the better purchase.

It remains to be seen, of course. As things are, the third phase in the evolution of programmed learning still leaves us in a learning situation which is largely restricted to verbal, written instructions and verbal, written responses. We are still at the silent stage of the industry and the art. With the advent of synchronized audio-visual adjuncts to computerized programmes we are a step nearer the all-talking, all-colour, all-everything stage, but still far short of anything approaching a multi-media communication system.

Yet such a system must be the logical outcome.

If we follow our paradigm for programmed instruction as it is represented by two-person interaction then the ideal teaching machine is a tutor. The tutor would be a machine of great complexity, a machine that could take into consideration the peculiarities of the individual student and modify its own behavior, its own functioning, in order to work most effectively with that particular student. The tutor would be an experimenter who had enough time to differentiate the behavior of all of his subject organisms, even where that behavior was composed of a large body of information and where the time required for its assimilation might consume years. This would be an expensive device. An approximation of this complex device is the picture of the ideal teacher that Galanter gives us (Galanter 1959). Galanter proposes a mechanism that would tax the capabilities of some of our most advanced computers. The machine he proposes is possible; with certain modifications it exists today. It is as expensive, and perhaps more expensive, than a flesh-and-blood tutor would be. Both of these examples make the point that one of the limitations of a teaching machine must inevitably be its cost. The economics of programmed instruction provide us with one of the most interesting facets of the entire business, both from the standpoint of feasibility and from the standpoint of the probable course of development of the field. In a way, what Galanter proposes is a Turing Machine.* The Turing Machine is a device whose operation is indiscriminable from the operation of a human. We are not, as Turing was, concerned with whether or not the machine thinks. We are concerned with the capabilities of its responding to the behavior of the student as a human teacher can respond. Is the machine capable of modifying itself to correct errors, to change the pace, to alter the subject matter in response to the needs and abilities of the learner? The human being is capable of this. A machine can be built that also is capable of this.[18]

Can be and will be. On that score there need be no doubt. The engineering obstacles are not so formidable that they cannot be overcome by an electronics industry which is already well into its stride and on the look-out for fresh fields to conquer. The economic obstacle remains, but even in three or four years since the above passage was penned the prospects have become distinctly less prohibitive. Machine technology is all-set to forge ahead. Whether the same can be said for the techniques which the programmers have striven so methodically and so patiently to refine is another matter. But if the crying need is for a prescriptive theory of instruction (and educationists keep saying that it is), at least let it be acknowledged that the programmers have done more than most to produce one, and that thanks to them its outlines, however glimmering, now begin to be discernible.

* Cf. A. M. Turing 'Can a Machine Think?' *Mind*, 1950.

REFERENCES

1 Robert M. Gagné *The Conditions of Learning*, pp. 281–2, Holt, Rinehart and Winston, 1965

2 W. Kenneth Richmond *Teachers and Machines*, p. 32, Collins, 1965

3 W. A. Deterline 'Learning Theory, Teaching and Technology', *Audio-Visual Communication Review*, **13**, No. 4, 1965

4 Patrick Meredith 'Toward a Taxonomy of Educational Media', *Audio-Visual Communication Review*, **13**, No. 4, 1965

5 Sidney Pressey 'Teaching Machines (and Learning Theory) Crisis' *Journal of Applied Psychology*, **47**, pp. 1–6, 1963

6 Norman Crowder 'Programmed Instruction Compared with Automated Instruction', *Trends in Programmed Instruction*, pp. 29–30, ed. Ofiesh and Meierhenry, DAVI, NEA and NSPI, 1964

7 W. R. Uttal 'On Conversational Interaction', *Trends in Programmed Instruction*, p. 185, ed. Ofiesh and Meierhenry, DAVI, NEA, and NSPI, 1964

8 Norman Crowder 'Programmed Instruction compared with Automated Instruction', p. 30, *Trends in Programmed Instruction*.

9 R. F. Mager *Preparing Objectives for Programmed Instruction*, Fearon, 1962

10 R. F. Mager, loc. cit., p. 53

11 R. F. Mager, loc. cit., p. 47

12 R. F. Mager, loc. cit., p. 53

13 R. F. Mager 'Setting Objectives for Programmed Instruction' (transcript of LCC lecture course for teachers, 28 Jan., 1964)

14 R. F. Mager 'The Acquisition of Knowledge', *Psychological Review*, **69**, pp. 355–65, 1962

15 R. Glaser 'Components of the Instructional Process', *Educational Technology*, p. 69, ed. De Cecco, Holt, Rinehart and Winston, 1964

16 Lawrence M. Stolurow 'Implications of Current Research and Future Trends', *Journal of Educational Research*, **55**, pp. 519–27, 1962

17 James A. Jordan, Sr. 'Socratic Teaching', *Harvard Education Review*, **33**, pp. 96–104, 1963

18 Edward J. Green *The Learning Process and Programmed Instruction*, pp. 128–9, Holt, Rinehart, and Winston, 1963

CHAPTER EIGHT

Outlines for a New Pedagogy

The chapter heading is pure bravado, of course. What follows, if not entirely abortive, is fated to have a dying fall. 'For the educationist it is an age of great expectations', we wrote earlier. 'Unfortunately, in the absence of a viable theory of instruction, it is not clear how we can live up to them.' Nothing would be more satisfying than to bring this book to a triumphant close by demonstrating that such a theory has at last been formulated and is now ready to be put into everyday practice, but at the moment this cannot be done. Many would even question the possibility of its being done in the foreseeable future.

> We cannot speak of 'the Science of Education'. 'Science' means not merely a hope but an achievement. We have no sufficiently organized body of educational facts and laws to warrant the term. Also it is not quite obvious what we should expect from such a science. If it were simply to represent a systematic description and interpretation of education as it *is* there might even be a temptation to use it in order to limit our conception of what *might* be. If, on the other hand, it were regarded as *prescriptive* we should have crossed the rather vague boundary between science and technology and should therefore speak of 'Educational Technology'. This likewise is in the future.[1]

If this is the considered opinion of forward-thinking scholars – and it comes from the editorial of the first issue of an international journal which is not ashamed to call itself *Educational Sciences* – it seems that the only sensible course is to bow to it.

Yet in all its guises, programmed learning represents an attempt to develop a technology of instruction. The curriculum reform movement, likewise, as witnessed in the new mathematics, team-teaching, and so on, stresses the need for a more systematic theory of instruction. Apart from sharing the same distrust of traditional methods and a liking for innovation, what do the two have in common? How, if at all, does a technology of instruction differ from a theory of instruction? Is it that they are related in the sort of way that legislature and executive are in government or as pure and applied branches are in science?

In saying that a technology is science-based we mean, among other things, that it is grounded on a thorough grasp of the principles behind the processes with which it deals; but as a general rule it seems fair to say that the accent is primarily placed upon the processes themselves rather than upon the principles which make them possible. By contrast, preoccupation with principles is fundamental for the educational theorist, which explains the fact that the curriculum reformers are often accused of thinking about the whole problem of instruction while the programmers have been busy doing something about it.

Now there are two ways of looking at educational principles. One sees them as absolute and immutable, holding good at all times and in all places. The other insists that they are relative, that they evolve and have a life of their own, a life that is implicated in the process of change. The modern spirit being pragmatic, the popular tendency is to favour the second viewpoint and to regard the first with indifference, not to say impatience. Hard-headed teachers and down-to-earth students for the most part share the opinion that the place for courses on 'Principles and Theory' is the lecture-theatre not the classroom, and that more often than not the content of such courses is so many words, words, words – airy talk which if not entirely out of this world is too far removed from it to win their interest and personal commitment. To their way of thinking, the truths propounded are no better than truisms, too nebulous as generalizations to have more than an indirect bearing on the work in hand. Forms without substance, they complain. The educational studies they prefer are the ones they can get their teeth into – the solid stuff of psychology and methodology. As for more fundamental issues, their attitude is akin to that of contemporary philosophy, which is only now, and reluctantly, coming round to the admission that there can be no permanent moratorium so far as the age-old, unanswered questions about the human condition are concerned – and even here, most of them would rather have a re-hash of the 'Ideas of the Great Educators' – *The Republic* and all that – than the fare served up to them by their present mentors, presumably because a historical context is better than none. In general, however, the feeling seems to be that educationists might do worse than take a leaf out of the book of Decision Theory, where the choice is never between abstract principles as such but between the ways these principles operate in a given situation.

They may be right. It is no accident that textbooks entitled *Principles of Education* are no longer written. Without necessarily accepting the gravamen of Professor D. J. O'Connor's charge (in his *Introduction to the Philosophy of Education*) which is, bluntly, that most, if not all, of the literature purporting to deal with educational theory is mere windbaggery, it is evident that this literature must have been lacking in several important respects, otherwise it could not have given rise to the mood of dissatisfaction now prevailing.

In what respects? While there can be no agreeing with O'Connor that the only acceptable model for an educational theory must be a scientific one if, by 'scientific', we mean a model based exclusively on the natural sciences, we are surely entitled to expect that any theory worth the name will serve three functions. First, it will be prescriptive, laying down in general terms a course of action and the conditions under which it has to be followed. Second, it will be predictive, indicating the outcome of that course of action. Third, it will be explanatory, capable of verifying the hypotheses on which its prescriptions and predictions rely.

And if it is too much to ask that the theory would emulate the methods of operational research, i.e. as a quantitative study and

N

evaluation of the process of instruction, involving machines and the men who use them, it would, at the very least, be capable of formulating questions and answers which were related to *observable* phenomena.

If, now, we ask what has been chiefly lacking in traditional theory the short answer must be that it was too content to remain descriptive. In considering its stock topics – 'discipline', 'Nature and Nurture', 'transfer of training', 'general and special aims', and the rest – it offered no firm guide-lines for the practitioner to follow. Its hypotheses were rarely working hypotheses, its precepts too tenuous to be serviceable.

> In any profession, practice must find its eventual justification in some body of established, organised and coherent body of theory. In this respect it may be thought that teachers suffer from a certain dis-advantage in that the theories at their disposal are neither very well organised nor particularly coherent. At the highest level of discourse these theories tend to lose themselves in philosophical abstruseness; at the lowest, they degenerate into small-talk about the tricks of the trade. The disadvantage arises not so much from the diversity of many different educational theories (and their failure to agree among themselves) as from the lack of definition in the middle sections of their spectrum. It is as though they had little or nothing to offer the broad mass of teachers who are not content to think of themselves merely as honest journeymen – the glass-blowers of the profession – and who have no pretensions to the role of the philsopher-king and the creative genius – the symphony writers. The rank and file, there-fore, can hardly be blamed if at times they feel envious of members of other professions whose work is conducted on more clear-cut lines. As they see it, theory is the soft centre, not the hard core around which their everyday practice revolves.[2]

Plainly, we do not have such a hard core. At the same time, we know what the requirements are, and here and there we can point to fragments of the theory which are already in place. Assembling them into a coherent whole is not going to be easy, and any verbal enunciation of the theory must, as yet, be in the nature of a raid on the inarticulate. To see in them the outlines for a new pedagogy may seem pretentious and would certainly be over-presumptuous were it not for the urgency of the need.

What we are groping towards is the kind of theory which will be capable of satisfying the threefold criteria of prescription, prediction, and explanatoriness. As a guide to teaching and curriculum planning it will accordingly be quite distinct from any so-called learning theory. The latter is essentially interpretive, being chiefly concerned to investigate and explain what happens *during* the act of learning. By contrast, a theory of instruction would be concerned with the prerequisite conditions and causes which ensure that learning takes place. To that extent, while it would not be above drawing on the findings of the learning theorists, it would not make the mistake of supposing that the solution of pedagogical problems can be left to the psychologists.

Such a theory, again, would be comprehensive, embracing far more than the techniques of imparting information and skills; it would have something to say about the affective as well as the cognitive domain, and might, indeed, be more appropriately dubbed a theory of pedagogy. So to designate it seems both apt and timely, for one of the useful purposes the theory would serve would be to discriminate between those aspects of the total culture which can and need to be transmitted via the formal agency of schooling and those which either cannot or do not need to be transmitted in this way. Another purpose would be to indicate the ways in which the apparent conflict between 'child-centred' and 'subject-centred' methods of teaching can be resolved, and to demonstrate just how, when, and why the two approaches can best be combined. Above all, the theory would be in keeping with the enlarged concept of educability which recent developments have thrust upon us, and would help to validate it by underlining the crucial importance of environmental influences and by indicating the ways in which these can be brought under rational control in the shaping of behaviour. The theory would be normative in the sense that it laid down established criteria and stated the conditions for satisfying them.

All of which, advisedly, is written in the future conditional.

As its leading proponent, Bruner takes the position that the kind of theory that is needed is, at best, putative; and that the most that can be done in our present state of knowledge is to offer short notes towards its definition.[3] In doing so, however, it seems that he is either being unduly modest or unnecessarily gloomy. A glance at the main elements of the theory of instruction, which he lists under the headings of [1] Predispositions, [2] The Structure of Knowledge, [3] The Sequence of Learning, and [4] Consequences, immediately prompts the comment that these correspond more or less exactly with the four aspects of programmed learning discussed in the previous chapter – i.e. Entering Behaviour (pre-test, subordinate capabilities, etc), Instructional Goals (learning-objectives, task analysis, etc), Instructional Procedures (linear, branching, computer-assisted and student-controlled sequencing of information and instructions), and Performance Assessment (post-test, 'knowledge of results', etc). From this it seems safe to infer that the curriculum reformers and the programmers, while pursuing different lines, are converging in the same directions and arriving at broadly the same conclusions. The same can be said of the work being done in the field of developmental psychology. Despite wide differences in background and aims there is a surprising measure of agreement between all three.

Moreover, even a cursory inspection of the list suggests that the desiderata are outweighed by the wealth of available data for the creation of the master theory which Bruner envisages. The real difficulty arises not so much from the fact that we know what the theory would be about but lack the requisite knowledge to give it effective expression, as from the fact that the relevant evidence is fragmented, scattered about all over the campus of educational literature and has yet to be fitted together. Only a concerted effort on the part of all concerned – teachers, academics, methodologists, programmers, psychologists, and social scientists (not forgetting the cultural anthropologist), can act as a catalyst to speed its formulation; and there seems to be little likelihood of this sort of get-together being brought about in Britain at the present time. In the USA, where the sense of urgency is greater and inter-disciplinary co-operation more easily arranged, a follow-up on the Woods Hole Conference might conceivably do the trick.

At any rate, the agenda for such a meeting of minds is clear enough. The points for discussion can be set out, however summarily, under the headings suggested in Bruner's essay 'Toward a Theory of Instruction'.

PREDISPOSITIONS

Teaching – Begin Here, says a popular book-title. Unfortunately, it is just here more than at any other stage in the educational process that the teacher finds himself in the dark. Easy enough to state the hypotheses:

1] That the capacity for learning is enormous in the earliest years of life and tends to decrease with advancing age

2] That formal instruction becomes feasible as soon as the child acquires articulate speech, and that the possibilities at the pre-school stage remain largely unexplored

3] That the kind of learning resulting from formal instruction is only part of the total life experience

4] That both the quantity and quality of learning depend to a great extent upon previous experiences, and that as a consequence

5] To be fully effective, instruction must begin with an informed awareness of the frame of reference which the individual brings to the learning situation.

But these are scarcely helpful. No one denies that it is desirable for the teacher to know as much as possible about his pupils before he meets them. Whether we refer to them as attitudes, mental sets, subordinate capabilities, or simply motivation, these are the *givens* – take them or leave them – the difficulty being that, to begin with, the teacher usually has only the roughest idea as to what they are and has to discover them as he goes along. The language of the sub-culture, the inter-personal relations of family

N 2

life, the play activities fostered in the home, the peer-group and the neighbourhood, the early identifications with this or that personality type – these and a host of other influences combine to decide the ways in which the child is to become the father of the man. Invariably, their massive influence has been brought to bear long before the teacher appears on the scene.

To say that they are beyond his control, however, is not to admit that they need always be beyond his ken. Still, vastly more attention will have to be paid to the approach work to formal education – propaedeutics – before the gross uncertainties which the teacher has to face are removed. As things are, he has no option but to accept a gift horse and make the best of a bad job. More sensitive diagnostic tests, together with a clearer appreciation of the prerequisites – levels of understanding, subordinate capabilities, etc – in different subjects will, presumably, help to make the choice of starting-point less chancy. Teacher-training, too, might help more than it does at present in introducing students to procedures for the detection not only of levels of scholastic attainment but also of levels of feeling and aspiration. In the long run it may well turn out that computer-assisted instruction can detect idiosyncracies and make the necessary adjustments for individual differences more speedily and more accurately than a human being can hope to do.

There remains the strong possibility, of course, that the ideal of finding the appropriate starting-point for each and every pupil is unattainable. Not feasible, and not eminently desirable, either, it may be thought. To the extent that predispositions mostly elude the teacher's control it seems that there is nothing much he can do about them. If so, a theory of instruction must recognize the limitations placed upon it, for in so far as intellectual development is pre-determined it is clearly not the stuff of pedagogy. Pedagogy is not paideia. Hence the need for the third of our hypotheses. In life as it is lived, and not only at the pre-school stage, a great deal of learning is acquired in ways which are non-deliberate, wholly or partly unconscious and to say the least of them obscure.

If the neurologists are right, deprivation of certain sense stimuli in early infancy produces chemical changes in the brain tissues with resultant adverse effects in behaviour, some of which are apparently irreversible. In much the same way that imprinting can induce a newly hatched gosling to follow a most unlikely looking foster parent for the rest of its life, so the infant's educability can be permanently distorted if he is not exposed to the 'right' kind of experiences at the 'right' time. Thus, the child who has not acquired the speech habits which are looked upon as *de rigueur*, or whose play-activities have failed to provide him with opportunities for familiarizing himself with spatial and geometric designs will almost certainly be handicapped when it comes to the formal learnings expected of him in school. Still more serious, his whole attitude to education may be hopelessly prejudiced. As Bruner observes, the luck-dominated mentality of the lower working class (so starkly revealed by some of Jackson and Marsden's Marburton interviewees) provides the educator with one of his toughest nuts – and one which no prescriptive theory has so far come near to cracking.

It will be noted that the ethical question concerning the 'right' kind of experience and its choice has been left open. A theory of instruction cannot evade the necessity of making value-judgements, but the first and most important, surely, should be that so far as possible the upbringing of the young should not be left to chance. To rely on womanly intuition or, worse, guess-work is inexcusable.

How far a theory of instruction would underline the importance of 'catching them young' (and how it would need to defend itself against the charge of giving *carte blanche* to social engineering if it did), is perhaps better left to conjecture. Two things it would certainly do. One would be to differentiate between school-bound learning and the kinds of non-deliberate learning which stem from the culture itself. The other would be to provide a clearer explanation of the nature and extent of individual differences, and in doing so enable the teacher to treat each and every pupil according to the cognitive–affective stage of development which he had reached.

THE STRUCTURE OF KNOWLEDGE

So far not so good, admittedly – a theory which can only offer a few barren hypotheses under the heading 'Predispositions' scarcely sounds promising. Mercifully, it looks as though the theoretical contribution as regards the structure of knowledge may amount to a genuine breakthrough in practice. Briefly stated, the hypothesis is that whatever the subject happens to be, and regardless of its 'difficulty', a way can be found of cutting it down to size, reducing it to a set of basic concepts which constitute its essential framework. Once this framework has been found the complexities and intricacies of subject-matter within the field are greatly simplified. The learner can find his way around the field more easily and see just where, how, and why the bits of information he gathers fit – bits and pieces which would otherwise tend to seem trivial, irrelevant, or accidental. The framework is invaluable in clearing the ground and removing the impedimenta to learning, and for that reason alone is economic of effort. It is also productive in that it enables fresh combinations of ideas to be made and facilitates transfer of training to other fields. In setting forth the objectives at the outset it enhances the spirit of inquiry by ensuring that the learner knows where he is going.

This principle of parsimony is by no means original. It is implicit in the Comenian intention to teach 'all things to all men'. A good example of it is to be found in the 'four great novel ideas' which Whitehead listed as being characteristic of nineteenth-century theoretical science – the idea of physical activity pervading the whole of space, the idea of atomicity, the idea of the conversion of energy, and the idea of evolution. Another example of its ruthless application to curriculum reform is to be seen in Chemical Bond Approach Project, which centres upon a single idea. According to this, the making and breaking of ties between atoms *is* chemistry, and everything in the course follows from, and hinges upon, an understanding of this one idea.

Preoccupation with the problem of structure has been forced upon educationists by the explosion of information. Particularly in the natural sciences, the exponential growth of knowledge has necessitated the adoption of conceptual schema which serve to make mass data more manageable and classifiable. With more and more needing to be learned and standards of attainment rising as fast as they are it is only natural that educationists should feel impelled to address themselves to the task of finding ways and means of shedding the load which the school-child has to carry in the second half of the twentieth century. On the one hand it is more obvious nowadays than ever before that not everything can be learned, on the other the demands of general education can be satisfied with nothing less than a broad grasp of essentials in a number of fields.

In this situation is it any use appealing to Turing's Theorem: 'Provided a problem is well defined its complexity can be broken down into a set of simpler operations'? Is it realistic to suppose that there is always a way of rendering down difficult subjects so as to make them readily assimilable by all?

The advocates of programmed learning are convinced that it can be done. So are the pioneers of curriculum reform. Neither pretends that it is going to be easy. Both can point to solid achievements as proof of their contentions, either to actual instructional devices or to syllabuses and textbooks designed to make it easier for the learner to find his way through the maze of facts and figures in which he might otherwise lose himself. Both acknowledge that it calls for an infinite capacity for taking pains, but that given the necessary persistence and ingenuity the job of creating order out of chaos is well worth doing, and one which has to be done if we are to have any chance of coping with the extraordinary proliferation of knowledge in all its forms in the modern world.

If there is a difference between the efforts of the programmers and those of the new curriculum planners it is that the latter have concentrated on the problem of *selection* – streamlining the content of the old courses, cutting out the lumber to make room for more up-to-date subject-matter – while the former have concentrated on the problem of *definition* – task analysis and the statement of precise objectives. Of the two, the second deserves to be seen as the more significant contribution. Possibly the most useful service which programmed learning has performed is that of forcing teachers to think hard – much harder than most of them have been accustomed to thinking in the past – about what exactly it is that they are trying to do. The easy-going belief that connoisseurship skills and critical thinking can only be conveyed by guess-and-by-God methods has been rudely shaken by the successful application of some of the latest programming techniques, which have gone a long way towards confirming the view that provided he is clear-sighted about the objectives the learner can be trusted to look after himself.

As we shall argue in another connexion, a measure of uncertainty is a necessary pre-condition for any purposeful inquiry. The point is that this uncertainty should never be associated with the task itself. The advantage of making plain the skeleton framework on which the subject-matter arranges itself is that it virtually rules out methods of presentation which create the impression that the outcome of the task is highly dubious and can only be arrived at, if at all, by hit-or-miss – an impression which is bound to be discouraging.

Stones puts the matter in a nutshell:

> Before attempting to introduce the children to a new type of problem the teacher must scrutinize the concepts involved, attempt to analyse them and isolate the essential components. The components are then presented in a graded sequence so that the pupil can see these basic units clearly and work with them. The teacher should also make clear to the pupils the way in which the sub-units of the problem are interconnected. That is, he so arranges the material that its structure is clear to the pupil. When he does this the pupil gets an overall view of the problem and through seeing its structure is able to work more rapidly and accurately than if he were left to grapple with different aspects of the problem presented in an apparently arbitrary way.[4]

Once again, however, we are brought back to the objection that some subjects lack any obvious structure and that in these cases the task of instruction is singularly ill-defined. The triumph of mathematics is that it is 'thought moving in the sphere of complete abstraction', which explains why it can be reduced to a set of basic postulates which give unity and coherence to the field of study. Literary, philosophical, and aesthetic studies, on the other hand, have a way of refusing to be pinned down, emphatically not the kind of subjects which permit of the objectives being written on the back of an envelope. In any case, teachers of the humanities will ask, is it not an illusion to suppose that the elucidation of the underlying structure in a subject field, supposing that there is such a thing, will be itself make learning easier? Is it not a fact that the 'New Mathematics', allegedly the perfect exemplar of a subject which lends itself to structural analysis, has run into trouble for this very reason, and that the average pupil finds it rather more difficult to comprehend?

That the elucidation of structure will not, in itself, solve all the problems of instruction may be conceded. At the same time, this does not absolve teachers of subjects like English, history, art, and religious instruction from the duty of doing what they can to bring their objectives into sharper focus and to make them known to their pupils. To say that their subjects lack obvious definition must not be used as an excuse for muddling through, for all it means is that in their case the task analysis is that much more difficult, not that it is impossible. If anything, the onus on them to find the missing rationale is the greater for that very reason.

Until it is disproved, therefore, the working hypothesis must be that any subject can be broken down into its essential components, each of which is distinct from, and at the same time interrelated with, the others. These sub-tasks are the mediators of the final performance. Once they are defined the order in which they need to make their appearance and the ways in which they depend upon each other become clearer. In a sense, then, the problem of structure is one and the same problem as that finding the appropriate sequence of learning, to which we turn next.*

* For a further discussion of the connexion between *structure* and *sequence* see Appendix.

THE SEQUENCE OF LEARNING

Here again we are reminded of the Comenian axioms: 'Nature proceeds step by step', and 'Nature observes a suitable time'. Only now, instead of paying lip-service to them, techniques for translating the axioms into practice are at last becoming available.

The notion of sequence has a twofold implication. [1] It implies that every subject has its own peculiar structure, its own internal regularities, principles, rules, laws, etc, and that these can be arranged in order so as to form a hierarchy. [2] It implies the existence of different levels of understanding appropriate to different stages of growth and mental development.

The second is the implication we have in mind when we speak of a developmental approach to teaching. In the past it has given rise to a number of tentative theories of instruction, e.g. Whitehead's three stages of Romance, Precision, and Generalization. It may be that Bruner's 'Enactive', 'Iconic', and 'Symbolic' levels of knowing are no better than a rehash of the same general theory.* It may also be the case that at present no theory can hope to do more in the way of prescription than to restate the hoary old maxims about working from the concrete to the abstract, from particular instances to general conclusions, induction to deduction and so *ad nauseam*. If so, it will earn no acclaim from anyone.

At the same time the hypothesis that any subject, no matter how abstruse, can be rendered intelligible to any child at any stage provides a clue of inestimable worth. The fact that at the enactive level the child knows how to balance himself on a see-saw is the guarantee that, provided the teacher goes about it in the right way, he can be raised to the symbolic level of understanding Newton's Law of Moments. The secret of finding the 'right way' lies in making explicit what, initially, is implicit in the child's experience.

* Z. P. Dienes, likewise, propounds a three-stage theory:
1] a preliminary, free-play stage;
2] a more closely structured, rule-bound play stage;
3] a conceptual, 'practice' stage.

The 'way' is dictated partly by the requirements of the internal logical structure of the subject itself, and partly by the pacing and timing of instruction to suit requirements which may be called maturational. As regards the importance of sequence in this second sense, it seems that curriculum planning, strongly influenced by the 'child-centred' school of thought and supported by the findings of Piaget and his associates, has favoured the developmental approach, while the programmed learning movement has been more concerned to interpret sequence in terms of the systematic presentation of information and instruction. On the whole, this apparent discrepancy between the aims of the new curriculum planners and the programmers is not regrettable, for although on the face of things it may seem that they figure in the roles of the Herbartians and the Froebelians only in modern dress, the two sides are looking at the problem of sequence from different angles. The two approaches are complementary and each stands to gain from the other. One labours to find the inherent step-by-stepness in the subject-matter, the other to ascertain the 'suitable time'.

Latterly, the two sides have showed signs of drawing closer together. Programmed learning, certainly, has advanced from its original, doctrinaire addiction to small steps and fixed sequences. While it has not backed down on its insistence on the need for graded practice accompanied by knowledge of results, it is much more disposed to agree that there is a place for open-ended inquiry – hunches, leaps in the dark, intuitions – as well as for the kind of bitty accretion which characterizes the learning process in a typical linear programme. Learning as problem-solving is now seen to be not simply a progression in a straight-forward linear dimension but rather as a progression from lower to higher orders of accomplishment, beginning at the lowest level with simple conditioning, rising to concept formations, thence to combinational principles which can be used to find the solution. Just as there are horses for courses, therefore, different types of programmes are needed. In some cases, mechanical arithmetic for instance, conditioning by means of fixed sequencing and tight control over the learner's responses may be in order, in others not. For the *avant-garde* of the movement, as we have seen, the inclination is to delegate the responsibility for finding the appropriate sequence to the learner himself. Some interesting experiments have been done, too, on lines very similar to those followed by the proponents of the so-called 'Spiral Curriculum', albeit with inconclusive results.

In the 'Spiral Curriculum', instead of the subjects being taught discretely, a variety of subjects is presented simultaneously, as an amalgam, and continuously revised and reviewed at subsequent stages and at higher levels. The argument is that in the teaching of general science, say, no one is certain whether biology should come before physics and chemistry, or even in the case of physics whether heat, light, and sound are best treated in that order.* Seeing that mental growth is continuous why not try to cater for as many aspects of general science as are thought necessary at one and the same time, reviewing them at successive stages of development? If biology alone, or physics alone, is taught over a period of a year or more, how do we know that psychological opportunities are not being missed – and how do we know that what is learned in an isolated section of the field will connect later on with another section? If it is possible to plot the logical sequence of presentation in a single subject on a flow chart may it not eventually be possible to decide the psychological order of events for the curriculum as a whole?

That we are a long way off producing satisfactory answers to these questions, particularly the last one, has to be freely admitted. In the experiment reported by Reynolds and Glaser two matched groups of American high school pupils were assigned to two

* This uncertainty as to the best starting-point for a course of study is well illustrated by the confused state of affairs in university entrance requirements. Klaus Boehm makes the point that: 'Most physics departments will require A-level passes in physics and mathematics; most departments of town planning will expect undergraduates to start from scratch. If you read philosophy at a university you start as it were on page 1; if you read history you *must* start on page 593. Why?' (*University Choice*, p. 13, Penguin Books, 1966.)
Why, indeed?

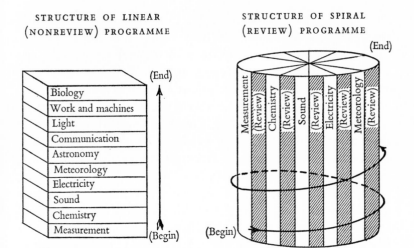

STRUCTURE OF LINEAR
(NONREVIEW) PROGRAMME

STRUCTURE OF SPIRAL
(REVIEW) PROGRAMME

(End)

Biology
Work and machines
Light
Communication
Astronomy
Meteorology
Electricity
Sound
Chemistry
Measurement

(End)
(Begin)

Measurement
(Review)
Chemistry
(Review)
Sound
(Review)
Electricity
(Review)
Meteorology
(Review)

(Begin)

FIG 10   Illustration of linear (nonreview) and spiral (review) programming formats as used in the general science programme. Constructed at the Programmed Learning Laboratory, University of Pittsburgh, 1961

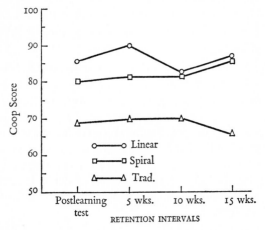

FIG 11   Retention curves for linear, spiral, and traditional groups over a 15-week period (fixed learning time). From J. H. Reynolds and R. Glaser, 'Effects of Linear and Spiral Programming upon Amount and Variability Theory', *Educational Technology*, p. 168, Holt, Rinehart and Winston

different programming formats, one working through a series of ten separate linear programmes, beginning with measurement and ending with biology, the other with a spiral programme on general science covering the same material. As might have been expected in view of the relatively short duration of the experiment, little or no difference was detectable in the long-distance retention scores of the two groups, but if only as a small beginning the experiment is interesting as evidence of the programmer's determination to push their investigations of the problem of sequence to greater lengths.

The developmental approach, while not standing idle, has undoubtedly benefited from the empirical methods of programmed learning. Readiness, for example, is no longer conceived in the *laissez-faire* fashion it was a few years ago. Instead of waiting upon maturation, as if the 'suitable time' could only come of its own accord, being set as it were by an internal clock, the policy now is to provide the environmental stimuli and conditions which will bring about the necessary changes in the learner. It is now recognized that readiness is much more a function of social and cultural factors than it is of purely psychological ones.

> 50,000 years ago there were men who were capable (under appro-
> priate conditions) of conducting a symphony orchestra, or of reading
> a paper to a learned society. There were no symphony orchestras or
> learned societies, not because of any purely psychological reasons,
> but because the processes of cultural accretion were at an early stage.
> That is, social and technological developments were too primitive to
> provide the appropriate conditions to nurture the psychological
> processes involving the very high levels of symbolic activity neces-
> sary in such complex skills as conducting or discoursing before
> learned societies.
>
> This argument faces the teacher with a fundamental question
> which cannot but influence his approach to teaching. Are we to
> consider that mankind has now reached a pinnacle of psychological
> development? Or that it is impossible for the general run of children
> to master increasingly complex mental skills? History would suggest
> that this is not so, but rather that in the past the potential was prob-

ably there but unrealised because the contemporary environment was inappropriate.[5]

The norms of scholastic attainment in any society reflect the ways in which that society orders and paces the upbringing of its children. These norms are relative and can be changed at will, depending as much upon economic factors as on anything else. Though comparative studies have so far failed to produce any firm measurements of the wide variations in the norms of different national systems of education, no one doubts that these variations exist. Judging only by the number of courses and examinations which the undergraduate has to take, the requirements for a first degree in Central European, Scottish, and Deep South, USA, universities suggest that they might be arranged in that ascending order of stiffness – always allowing, of course, for fluctuations in standard from institution to institution. Though he is likely to lose friends for saying so, the author's impression for what it is worth as an external examiner, is that the amount of work done and the level of intellectual prowess needed to gain the equivalent of a first-class honours BA award, say, at Charles University, Prague, is not always (or even normally) exceeded by a PhD candidate qualifying in some of the less reputable American state universities. Whether or not it is safe to infer from this that the educational norm of a country is an index of its affluence is an entirely different matter.

The point which cannot be underlined too strongly is that the extent of human capabilities cannot be fixed, depending as it does on the efficiency of instruction, which in turn depends upon its ordering and pacing. While it is not possible, as yet, to point to a 90 per cent success with 90 per cent of the population there is no longer any reason to query the hypothesis that higher all-round standards of achievement are within our grasp and that the whole learning process can be speeded up very significantly.

At the levels of simple conditioning, concept formation and the learning of principles the chances are that the careful sequencing of instruction will be better left to mechanical controls: the human nervous system is too shaky and liable to break down under the stress of the moment to be utterly trustworthy in discharging these lesser purposes. To say this should occasion neither surprise nor offence: after all, as motorists, we must agree that a set of traffic lights is less prone to error than a policeman on point duty at a busy intersection, and if this seems too trite an analogy there are plenty of others which might be adduced. It is at the higher levels where truly personal teaching takes over from the more formal procedures of instruction that the human touch, as it is called, enters its own.

CONSEQUENCES

All instruction ends by making itself unnecessary. It is a process whereby the learner is gradually weaned away from external, imposed disciplines to voluntary and responsible self-control. The dynamics of the process are supplied by the system of rewards and punishments operating formally in the educational system itself and less formally, but no less effectively, in social life.

If there is one issue on which a technology of instruction and a theory of instruction agree absolutely it is that nothing succeeds like success and that fear of failure is the direst threat to learning. The *funktionslust* which gives zest and relish to the classroom experience in Soviet schools, and which is commented on so favourably and enviously by most foreign observers, is an indispensable ingredient in any learning situation. That the recipe is a subtle one, owing more to the climate of opinion (i.e. the aspirations and expectations engendered in the society which the school serves) may be gathered from the fact that the methods and styles of presentation to be found in most classrooms in the USSR strike the same observers as being pedestrian, even old-fashioned.

For the programmers the key to the situation is to be found, in principle, in the feedback of information to learner and instructor alike – 'knowledge of results'. For the devotees of the New Mathematics, the New Science and that ilk the key word is 'inquiry'. It seems that, however, obliquely, both are hinting at the same meaning. It seems likely, too, that immediate confirmation and a low error-rate are appropriate to the lower-level learning processes, and that the use of open-ended, if-then propositions is increasingly to be recommended at the higher levels. As we have indicated, the notion that immediate confirmation of the correctness of responses automatically and invariably acts as a reinforcer must be reckoned suspect. But if the early programmers allowed themselves to be duped into thinking that the surest way of avoiding aversive behaviour was to rule out the possibility of error the fault was at least pardonable. To the extent that it rested on the conviction that learning needs to be pleasurable it was based on a sound insight. To the extent that it was satisfied with envisaging the learning process as a piecemeal affair it was guilty of a serious oversimplification. The afflatus of the Aha reaction, the sudden flash of recognition which occurs when principles are applied to the 'original' solution of a problem – what follows when the evidence has been presented and the invitation to consider the implications of the if-then question is accepted – is a heightened form of reinforcement which cannot be overlooked.

Once again, it is necessary to distinguish between lower and higher levels of learning. At the lower level, the imposition of rigid external controls and strict adherence to a systematic presentation of *information* must be considered legitimate and necessary: at the higher, the relaxation of controls and increased reliance on the learner's ability to draw his own conclusions from *instruction per se* (i.e. guidance, advice, etc) must be allowed for. Either way, we can be sure that the philosophy of testing-as-you-go works both ways, an intelligence service which ensures that the teacher, no less than the pupil, is constantly apprised of the progress he is making.

STYLES OF COMMUNICATION

Never let it be forgotten that teaching, too, has its Great Masters, the inimitable ones whose lineaments shine through history: Socrates, the professed know-nothing, whose cruel-to-be-kind cross-examinations reduced those who submitted to them to a state of intellectual collapse; Jesus, who spoke as one having authority; Pestalozzi, ill-favoured, often improperly dressed and apt to fly into a tantrum, whose ways with peasant children drew admirers from every country in Europe and from across the Atlantic.

How to account for the extraordinary power of these men? To proclaim that they were outstanding personalities explains nothing, unless it be that they were the kind of men who stand outside the boundaries of convention. Each is characterized by a humility as profound as it is irreproachable, by a simplicity of utterance which is oracular, above all by an unfailing spirit of charity capable of winning total commitment from those who sat at their feet. To hear them speak, even to be in their presence, was to become a disciple. Yet each remains an enigma.

As readers of St Augustine's *De Magistro* will recall, to ask what happens when we teach turns out to be a deceptively innocent-looking question. Whatever the form of words it takes, the answer is fated to be unsatisfactory. If we say that what happens is 'the conscious bringing about in others of certain desirable mental and dispositional changes by morally acceptable means',[6] then (leaving aside the begged questions in the definition) we have no alternative but to agree that members of most other professions – clergymen, actors, journalists, and doctors – are in some way or other engaged in teaching, in which case there is no possibility of setting up any general test of competence or of laying down any established criteria for good teaching. As Professor Bantock concedes, the prior question of what constitutes the process whereby someone teaches someone something is not in itself an empirical question.

It might appear from this that the duties assigned to the 'teacher' are quite specific, limited to the relatively narrow range of cognitive skills which we have in mind when we speak of 'school-bound learning'; and, in fact, in their less guarded moments, this is what the great majority of teachers admit to believing. 'I teach Latin – never mind about John' is the sum of their philosophy. Let the teacher stick to his last, which begins and ends as formal instruction. Yet educational theory, not to mention the law, has always demanded a great deal more, not least on the score of moral training and development. A theory of instruction which construed the teacher's task solely in terms of predispositions, structure, sequence, and consequences and had nothing to say about styles of presentation and the nature of the teacher–pupil relationship itself would leave out the heart of the matter. Even if it only leads to the conclusion that whether we call it an art, a science, or a technology, teaching is a highly mysterious affair, the attempt has to be made.

Let us begin again, then, watching our every word. What happens when we instruct?

'To instruct' is an active verb, 'to be instructed' passive. Evidently, the process of instruction presupposes an exchange between persons. It is an *ars cooperativa* and it is made possible by a process which we are accustomed to refer to as 'communication'. What happens, then, when we communicate? In our daily lives each of us communicates information, ideas, opinions, wishes, commands, attitudes, moods, and (every time we sneeze) even the germs of disease. Common to all these acts is the idea of something – information, meta-information, germs – being transmitted from one person, the sender, to another, the receiver. Thus, 'I told him the facts', 'I broke the news to him', 'I impressed upon him the need for action', 'I gave him a piece of my mind'. The fact that these verbal expressions can be classified as deliberate communications and that many non-verbal forms of communication cannot is immaterial. At the same time, it would be wrong to infer that all that happens (except possibly in the case of sneezing!) is a one-way transfer. Invariably, the sender communicates *with*, as well as *to*, the receiver. In order for the sender to transmit his message – get across the information, as we say – the receiver must be able to receive and interpret it, or, failing this, must be able to make known his inability to receive and interpret it. Language is the medium *par excellence*, but by no means the only one, which makes this interchange possible. Music, for example, is a more potent vehicle for the transmission of moods, and a nod or a look often a more immediate indication of intention than the second-order signals of words.

But whatever the medium used, the outcome of communication is the resolution of uncertainty, a communion of understanding and feeling in which both parties share.

What, then, invests this exchange with significance? As Bantock observes, 'A social act may differ in significance in accordance with penetrative depth of comprehension. Even when the general character of religious practices is recognised as such the "meaning" they may have for the believer can play quite a different role in the life of that believer from what they can in that of a non-believer. In the same way, the act of sex can "mean" anything from the semi-clinical ("relief of tension") to the semi-mystical ("She is all States, and all Princes, I . . .).'[7]

In this connexion, the mathematical concept of entropy as used in communication theory, is likely to prove as helpful as any. According to this,

> The amount of information conveyed by the message increases as the amount of uncertainty as to what message actually will be produced becomes greater. A message which is one out of ten possible messages conveys a smaller amount of information than a message which is one out of a million possible messages. The entropy of communication theory is a measure of this uncertainty, and the entropy, or uncertainty, is taken as the measure of the amount of information conveyed by a message from a source.[8]

The significance, in other words, varies according to the latitude of choice exercised by the sender. As the communication theorist calculates it: 'Specifying or learning the choice between two equally probable alternatives, which might be messages or numbers to be transmitted, involves one bit of information.'[9]

Are we to conclude from this that the significance of instruction decreases in proportion to the lucidity of its presentation, and that the kind of teaching which leaves little or nothing in doubt is inferior to the kind which leaves a great deal unexplained? If the *bit* really is what it claims to be, 'a universal measure of amount of information in terms of choice and uncertainty', what are we to think of the mode of learning in a typical linear programme where all the responses are of the true–false (one bit per frame) type? Or is it that the kind of information measured by the communication theorist is somehow different from the kind with which a theory of instruction has to deal?

It is true that communication theory grew out of the study of electrical communication, that it remains strongly mathematical, and has yet to demonstrate that it embraces all forms of human communication. At the same time it serves notice on us that a measure of uncertainty is indispensable. Without it there could be no point in deciphering the message, no meaningful inquiry.

Indispensable, yes, but how to strike a balance between the gratuitous and the incomprehensible? It has become one of the clichés of the Age of Anxiety to say that when all has been said and done, all the facts made known, there is still nothing to guarantee that a fatal breakdown of communication will not occur. There is a distressing tendency for the exchanges of words to result only in people talking past one another, and not only because of the snares inherent in the use of language. In industrial disputes and international conference tables the statements, arguments, and views put forward by one party make no impression on the other, either because the motives behind them are distrusted or because cross-cultural differences result in the lines of communication becoming hopelessly crossed. The same words do not signify the same things to both parties. In these circumstances uncertainty, far from enhancing the significance of what is said, breeds only distrust: interpretation becomes a guessing game in which the sender's honesty is never patent and cannot be taken as read.

Fortunately there is a way round the impasse. Even when the uncertainty reaches the point where it becomes intolerable there remain ways and means of communication which are not always conscious at the time, some of which might even be described as non-rational. 'Example', 'imitation', 'insight', 'identification', 'intuition', 'infection', 'contagion', and 'empathy' are some of the names we give them.

Says Sorokin,

Only through direct empathy . . . can we grasp the essential nature
and difference between a criminal gang and a fighting battalion,
between a harmonious and a broken family. . . . The same can be
said of the nature and differences of religious, scientific, aesthetic,
ethical, legal, economic, technological and other cultural value-
systems and their sub-systems. Without the direct living experience
of these cultural values they will remain terra incognita for our outside observer and statistical analyst.[10]

A theory of instruction must accordingly make adequate provision
for the affective side of learning. The polarities of communication
are not simply those of sender and receiver, they are also those in
which heart and head are engaged, of sentiment as well as concept.

Looked at in this way, it appears that there are two distinct
styles of presentation, one of which is mainly expository and
analytical, aiming at the imparting of 'knowledge', the other more
inferential and synthetic, aiming at a sensitive attention to, and
awareness of, 'experience'. The one leads to 'understanding', the
other to 'appreciation'. Broadly speaking (but only very broadly)
the two styles correspond to what we have known all along as
the teacher- or subject-centred approach – Herbartian pedagogy –
on the one hand, and the so-called child-centred doctrine on the
other. The placing of inverted commas round some of the words
used to differentiate between them indicates that 'thin partitions
do their bounds divide'. Since the two go hand in hand, comple-
menting each other, any attempt to tabulate the differences
between them runs the risk of serious over-simplification, a risk
which nevertheless has to be taken.

EXPOSITORY STYLE

1a] Sees communication mainly from the side of the sender.
2a] Concentrates on the imparting of information.
3a] Keeps the content and sequence of information under the control of the instructor.

INFERENTIAL STYLE

1b] Tries to see communication from the side of the receiver.
2b] Relies more on giving instructions which encourage self-directed inquiry.
3b] Delegates this control wherever and whenever possible.

4a] Allows the sequence to be determined by the requirements of the subject-matter.

4b] Makes allowance for the individual learner's psychological needs.

5a] Aims at the direct acquisition of cognitive skills – 'intellectual excellence'.

5b] Indirectly inculcates values and attitudes – 'moral excellence'.

6a] Uses positive statements – 'This is so', 'This is me telling you'.

6b] Prefers hypothetical statements – 'If this is so, then what?'

7a] Is openly didactic.

7b] Resorts to heuristic methods.

8a] Thinks of instruction as an additive process, advancing gradually step by step.

8b] Answers to a cyclical principle – the sudden apprehension of wholes.

9a] Appeals at all points to the learner's rationality.

9b] Engages the learner's sympathy.

10a] Believes that it is not safe to leave the learner to his own devices.

10b] Believes that under guidance the learner can look after himself.

Frankly, there is not one point in the list that the writer himself would not want to query or to quarrel with as being unnecessarily arbitary. Of them all, [9a] and [9b] look like being the most contentious.

At first blush, a theory which ventures to draw a distinction between rationality and sympathy may seem to be courting disaster, and will no doubt be received with derision in academic circles if nowhere else. So much the worse for those who deride it. For if there is one single attribute peculiar to master teachers throughout the ages, we know that it is an attribute which is not confined to the improving of men's intellectual accomplishments but one capable of capturing and holding the personal allegiance of their disciples. To acknowledge that there is more to instruction than a ribbon development of the brain, and that (as Bruner puts it) acts of knowing stem from the left hand as well as from the right is not to obfuscate and romanticize the issue but to bring it into the open where it belongs. It seems that in the last resort there is no substitute for the spirit of charity. Without it there may be mental discipline but not the discipline that comes of discipleship.

o

It is at this point more than at any other that the practicability of any theory of pedagogy is certain to be tested most severely. Time and again, new entrants to the teaching profession and students in training clamour for a positive lead in the matter of classroom management. Of all the personal problems that beset them this, apparently, is the one which worries them most. How to gain a hearing, let alone fire the enthusiasm of unruly adolescents? How to rouse the sullen, the apathetic, the rebellious ones? How to quell the incipient riot that always seems to be threatening? For that matter, how to defend oneself in the face of naked hostility?

So long as the circumstances in which school-bound learning are expected to take place remain unchanged the only proper course is to refrain from offering any sort of advice on these problems. A situation in which the teacher is mistrustful, half-afraid or fighting shy of his pupils and the pupils themselves for one reason or other at odds with their teacher is symptomatic of a deep-seated social malaise. In trying to diagnose it, the theorist cannot fail to note that the problems on both sides are personal, and that they are primarily emotional, not simply intellectual. He must also note that reasonably efficient instruction is always possible where sergeant-major methods are adopted, despite latent opposition. Having done so, he is bound to reach the conclusion that because of social changes these methods are inappropriate in the classroom situation as it exists today. The young will no longer stand for them. It is as though the gap between adulthood and immaturity had suddenly widened and deepened into an open rift. In McLuhan's view, the offspring of the television era are not to be thought of in terms of a rising generation as has been done hitherto – they belong to an entirely new breed.

The manipulators of mass media have latched on to this idea faster than the schools and adapted their styles of presentation accordingly. 'ITV TO SHOW GOD BY IDENTIKIT', a newspaper headline announces.[11] To deplore such tactics on the grounds of raw sensationalism is to miss the point. The crying need of the time is for styles of communication in the classroom which will at least vie in their impact and appeal with those to which young people are accustomed. It may be that this appeal, and the heightened emotional awareness that goes with it, cannot be encompassed within the walls of the classroom as we have it. It may be, too, that the impact which is needed is beyond the reach of ordinary mortals working single-handed. If so, some way of building it into a multi-media teaching machine may be the only answer. Abhorrent as it will be to many people, the thought has to be faced that a machine may prove to be a more efficient instrument for instruction, and a more sensitive one, than the men who design and operate it.

So, also, has the realization that the responsibility for learning anything rests ultimately with the learner himself. There is a paradox here, to be sure, and a wholesome one. On the right hand, the suggestion is that it is up to the instructor to do everything in his power to ensure that learning takes place, and that if things go wrong the fault is his: on the left, the contradictory suggestion is that the learner can look after himself. The contradiction cannot be dodged by saying that, of course, it all depends upon what is meant by efficient instruction – that if the purposes we have in mind are akin to those which the sergeant-major discharges so ably and vociferously then it will be necessary for the instructor to figure in a dominant role, whereas if the purposes are more subtle and personal the emphasis will shift towards the learner. Neither can it be avoided by saying that the choice between expository and inferential styles of teaching depends upon mental ages, the first being justified in the case of the very young, the second with older and more advanced pupils. Defenders of the *status quo* only pull the wool over their own eyes in seeing the continuous process of education as the embodiment of a three-stage cycle in which there is a steady progression from drum-it-into-them methods to self-rule. The cycle is not to be thought of chronologically. Sound pedagogy must arrange for both styles to be adopted simultaneously all along the line. There *is* no choice between them. If only for the sake of correcting the imbalance which centuries of teacher-dominated instruction have created, however, it looks very much as though the inferential style, as we have called it, is more in keeping with the present climate of opinion both inside and outside the schools. As levels of aspiration and expectation continue to rise it will become increasingly difficult to resist the learner's claim to be treated as an autonomous individual. To underline a point made earlier on, possibly the most chastening fact which emerges from a study of the history of education is that pupils have contrived to learn reasonably well in the past not because of the methods used but in spite of them. Worth pondering, too, is the fact that so many research studies report no significant differences in the results obtained from the adoption of some of the latest and most high-powered techniques of instruction. The biggest variable in the learning situation is the learner himself. Apart from that, all that can be said for certain is that the conditions for successful learning are now tolerably well known, and that, thanks to this, higher levels of attainment are accessible for an increasing number of children. Contemporary pedagogy should not rest content until the same can be said for all.

REFERENCES

1 Patrick Meredith Editorial, *Educational Sciences*, **1**, No. 1, February 1966.
2 W. Kenneth Richmond *Teachers and Machines*, p. 8, Collins, 1965
3 J. S. Bruner *Toward a Theory of Instruction*, Harvard University Press, 1966
4 E. Stones *An Introduction to Educational Psychology*, Methuen, 1966
5 Ibid.
6 G. H. Bantock *Values and Education*, p. 167, Faber, 1965
7 loc. cit.
8 J. R. Pierce *Symbols, Signals and Noise*, p. 79, Hutchinson, 1962
9 loc. cit.
10 P. A. Sorokin *Fads and Foibles in Modern Sociology*, pp. 159, 160, Regnery, 1956
11 *Daily Telegraph*, June 15, 1966

Structure and Sequence in Curriculum Planning

A practical illustration of the relationship between the structure of a field of knowledge and the sequence in which its content is presented may be seen in the Biological Sciences Curriculum Study.

As regards *structure*, it was decided that any course in biology would need to be organized round nine basic themes:

1] Change of living things through time – evolution
2] Diversity of type and unity of pattern of living things – taxonomy, speciation
3] Genetic continuity of life
4] Biological roots of behaviour
5] Complementarity of organism and environment – ecology
6] Complementarity of structure and function – morphology
7] Maintenance of life in the face of change – regulation and homeostasis
8] Science as inquiry
9] Intellectual history of biological concepts.

Themes 1–7 were thought of as defining the content, themes 8–9 as conveying the logical structure of the course.

The question then arose as to the *order* in which these themes could be presented most effectively and what the starting-point should be. In the event, three variant syllabuses were produced and tried out in high schools throughout the USA.

1] *The Blue Version* ('Molecules to Man') approaches biology at the molecular, biochemical level. The textbook retraces the story of evolution under the headings of: [1] Biology as the interaction of facts and ideas – science as inquiry, varieties of living things, the means of evolution, the origin of living things; [2] Evolution of the cell – the forerunners of life, chemical energy for life, master molecules, the biological code; [3] The evolving organism – light as energy for life, the evolved cell, cell theory, the multicellular organism; [4] Multicellular organisms: new individuals – reproduction and development; [5] Multicellular organisms: energy utilization – photosynthetic systems, transport systems, digestive systems, excretary systems; [6] Multicellular organisms: integrative systems, regulatory systems, nervous systems, muscular and skeletal systems, the integrated organism and its behaviour; [7] Higher levels of organization – populations, societies, and communities.

2] *The Yellow Version* ('Biological Science: An Inquiry into Life') starts with cell structure and incorporates the nine basic themes under the headings of: [1] Cells – introduction to biology, unit of structure in life cells, the search for a chemical 'key' to cell life, biochemistry, balance of energy in life, cell reproduction; [2] Micro-organisms – viruses, bacteria, fungi, and the balance of life; [3] Plants – evolution and diversity of plants, photosynthesis, life processes in plants; [4] Animals – the animal way of life, diversity among animals, life processes in animals; [5] Genetics – patterns of heredity, chromosome theory, genes and their action, genetics in populations of organisms; [6] Evolution – history of evolutionary theory, mechanisms of evolution, cultural evolution in man; [7] Ecology – population and communities, man and the balance of nature.

3] *The Green Version* ('High School Biology') begins the other way round, so to speak, and approaches the subject from the behavioural and ecological aspects. The sections of the textbook are as follows: [1] The biosphere dissected – the living world, individuals, populations and communities around diversity, plant diversity, microscopic life; [2] Patterns in the biosphere – life on land, life on inland waters, life in the seas, the history of life, the geography of life; [3] The individual dissected – the cell, the functioning plant, the functioning animal, reproduction and development, heredity; [4] Evolution, behaviour and man – mechanisms of evolution, behaviour, the human animal, man and the biosphere.

Approximately two-thirds of the core content is the same for all three versions, as is the level of attainment aimed at, yet in each case the approach to the nine basic themes, the emphases given them, and the order in which they make their appearance are essentially different. Although the final choice of sequence is still being worked out empirically by the BSCS project, its intimate connexion with the structure of the field is apparent.

Select Bibliography

Chapter 1
THE TEACHING REVOLUTION

ELVIN, H. L., *Education and Contemporary Society*, Watts, 1965
FRANKEL, C., *The Case for Modern Man*, Harper, 1956
MILES, M. B. (ed.), *Innovation in Education*, Teachers College, Columbia, 1964
MUMFORD, L., *Technics and Civilisation*, Routledge, 1934
RICHMOND, W. K., *Teachers and Machines*, Collins, 1964
STANLEY, W. O., *Education and Social Integration*, Teachers College, Columbia, 1964
Year Book of Education 1965: 'The Education Explosion'
Higher Education (Robbins Report): Appendix One, H.M.S.O., 1963

Chapter 2
THE CHANGING CONCEPT OF EDUCABILITY

BRUNER, J. S., *The Process of Education*, Harvard, 1960
GETZELS, J. W. and JACKSON, P. W., *Creativity and Intelligence*, Wiley, 1962
HUDSON, L., *Contrary Imaginations*, Methuen, 1966
VAIZEY, J., *Education for Tomorrow*, Pelican Books, 1966

Chapter 3
TEAM TEACHING

SHAPLIN, J. T. and OLDS, H. T., *Team Teaching*, Harper and Row, 1965

Chapter 4
THE NEW MATHEMATICS

DIENES, Z. P., *An Experimental Study of Mathematics Learning*, Hutchinson, 1964

WOOTON, W. (ed.), School Mathematics Study Group: *The Making of a Curriculum*, Yale, 1965

National Council of Teachers of Mathematics: 'The Revolution in School Mathematics', Washington, 1963

Chapter 5
FRESH APPROACHES IN THE TEACHING OF SCIENCE

BOULIND, H. F. (ed.), *Physics*, Longmans, Green and Penguin Books, 1966

DOWDESWELL, W. H. (ed.), *Biology*, Longmans, Green and Penguin Books, 1966

HALLIWELL, H. F. (ed.), *Chemistry*, Longmans, Green and Penguin Books, 1966

American Association for the Advancement of Science: 'The New School Science'

Chapter 6
ENGLISH AT THE CROSSROADS

HOLBROOK, D., *English for the Rejected*, Cambridge University Press, 1964

HALLIDAY, M. A. K., MCINTOSH, A., and STREVENS, P., *The Linguistic Sciences and Language Teaching*, Longmans, Green, 1964

Chapter 7
FROM AUDIO-VISUAL AIDS TO MULTI-MEDIA COMMUNICATION SYSTEMS

COULSON, J. E. (ed.), *Programmed Learning and Computer Based Instruction*, Wiley, 1962

GAGNE, R. M., *The Conditions of Learning*, Holt, Rinehart and Winston, 1965

MAGER, R. F., *Preparing Objectives for Programmed Instruction*, Fearon, 1962

MCLUHAN, M., *The Gutenberg Galaxy*, Routledge, Kegan Paul, 1962

MCLUHAN, M., *Understanding Media*, Routledge, Kegan Paul, 1966

OFIESH, G. D. and MEIERHENRY, E. C. (ed.), *Trends in Programmed Instruction*, D.A.V.I., National Education Association and National Society for Programmed Instruction, 1964

Chapter 8
OUTLINES FOR A NEW PEDAGOGY

BRUNER, J. S., *Toward a Theory of Instruction*, Harvard, 1966

Index